7-30-00

TRAILERS
How to Design & Build

Volume 1. BASICS

Robert Cornelius Jr.
333 E. Wheeling St.
Lancaster, OH - 43130
740-654-7774

TRAILERS

HOW TO DESIGN & BUILD

Volume 1. BASICS

by

M. M. SMITH, BSME

TECHNI-VISIONS
Downey, California

DEDICATED TO

the many welders whose stories
of woe in building trailers
touched my heart

TABLE OF CONTENTS

NOTES

This is at least the second or third major version of this book and hopefully the final version. After 14 years of writing, rearranging, drawing and calculating we have found that it will take three volumes to present this material. The first volume has six chapters which include most of the things people think about when they think about building a trailer. The 2nd and 3rd volumes cover calculations and other technical aspects which are also very much a part of building a trailer and often don't get included in the process. Frame strengths and towability are covered in **Volumes 2** and **3**. If you actually do intend to design and build your own trailer, reading and understanding all three volumes will help you understand many of the basics necessary to start and work through your project. The information in this series applies primarily to trailers under 7500-lbs gross capacity. Some may be applicable for larger trailers but an expert should be consulted.

Volume 1 has been divided into six chapters. Chapter 1 and 2 are introductory. Chapters 3, 4 and 5 cover components. Chapter 6 discusses the actual building and assembly, cutting, layout, welding and painting. Major suppliers are listed in the Appendix. If you have no place else to start searching, this is a good beginning. Other beginning ideas can include recreation areas where people use trailers. Find one you like and use it as a starting point. Use the cautions in these books to evaluate and improve upon that existing design. Do be cautious because some trailers aren't what they seem, as we discuss here.

This book is a record of my experience building trailers and is in no way "the Gospel." There are certainly other ways of doing it which are just as effective. The advantage of a book is that you have the choice of using the information or not. The disadvantage is that you often have no one to check the manner in which you choose to use the information. As a result it is difficult for us to take any responsibility for what you can create or what you do create. Remember this as you read or use the information contained here. Make sure it makes sense to you and to your situation. If you have any questions about it, be sure to consult with someone who has the necessary knowledge to help you.

ACKNOWLEDGMENTS

As with any book, it takes more than the author to complete it. And with a technical book of this nature, this step is especially important. In the beginning, Rich McCormack of Newport Press helped with the concept and initial formatting. Overall editing and finding of those infamous little errors was done by two trusted friends—Wendy Jo Block, a journalism expert and R.E. Williams, a technical expert in the field of engineering.

Typing the first draft of the manuscript (and a few thereafter) was the tedious doing of Delores McTaggart with an old fashioned typewriter. Finally in 1987 drafts were transferred to the MacIntosh computer. From there, the book began to take its present shape. Debbie West and Paulette Kelly tirelessly revised draft after draft on their own computers as the book was transformed into its present configuration. And now thousands of hours later with numerous corrections, additions and changes behind us we have a 100 page book which has grown to two volumes of almost 200 pages each.

Although the majority of drawings in this volume were done from my own knowledge, data for some was gathered from other sources. Especially helpful were the people at *Kruse Feed & Supply* in South El Monte, California who assisted me with weighing of alfalfa bales when I showed up with a scale. Comments on Chapter 3 were solicited from my friends at *Century Wheel & Rim*—Richard Starks, Gene DiSano and Jerry Milsap. The axle calculations in this same chapter were checked by Ken Foster, a structural engineer and Merle Bolden, a trailer engineer with *Century*. Wheels and tires for photographs were provided by Al Featherstone at *Industrial Tire Company*. And Dan Guinn of *D & G Welding* in Littlerock, California provided his plasma cutter and heliarc welder for photos used in Chapter 6.

And I certainly must thank all the torsion axle manufacturers for their assistance in providing information to make a thorough discussion of torsion axles possible. Norm Reynolds of *Torax* wrote a 5 page detailed letter about the benefits of torsion axles in general and more specifically the benefits of steel torsion axles. Don Boerger and Vic Rosengarten at *Henschen* were also extremely helpful in providing useful test data and general technical information in this area. Conversations with Vince Scott of *UCF* and Mike Platz of *AL-KO* rounded out the subject of torsion axles. Mike Platz also looked up and sent me a large amount of data and literature on mechanical brakes commonly used in Europe.

Ron Haase at *Dutton Lainson* provided accurate information on bearing protectors and an engineering drawing, included as an inset in one of the Figures in Chapter 3. John Bechtold of *Unique Functional Products* also took the time to discuss the benefits of bearing protectors and send photos and drawings.

Tom Kneiss of *Hammerblow Corporation* referred me to a distributor, *AgServ West* where John McKeon, Jr packaged and sent several heavy duty trailer jacks for the photographs in Chapter 5. Thom Perry and Julie Dunham from *Superwinch™* sent a chart describing methods of calculating winch strengths for use in Chapter 5. Charles Perry followed with an additional detailed letter providing information which has been added to this newer version.

Photography in general was largely my doing with many photos taken from files of vacations across the Southwest. Most product pictures were chosen from the IRD library of photos, which were also taken by the author. Some product photos were provided by *Hammerblow, Unique Functional Products* and *Dutton Lainson*. The *Mubea* ironworker photo shown in Chapter 6 was the courtesy of Steve Cashion of *Meyer Sheet Metal Machinery* in Los Angeles. As you can see it takes effort from many people to compile the information necessary to write a complete book. We must all be extremely grateful to these people (and I sure hope I haven't missed any), because they helped to fill in areas of the book that were weak or non existent. Luckily, my 18 year tour of duty in the trailer manufacturing business was instrumental in providing the foundation .

SAFETY FIRST, LAST & ALWAYS!

This book has been written to improve your safety and the safety of trailers in general—not decrease it. We believe that increased knowledge is a prime key to your building of a successful trailer. Bear in mind though that all the knowledge needed is NOT included here. There are so many aspects to a project like this, we can't possibly cover them all. This book contains few outright recommendations and is merely a list of specifications for items used to build a trailer. How you combine these parts and pieces is beyond our knowledge and control. Any trailer designs you concoct must be carefully considered and done with the entire system including the tow vehicle as part of your thinking. Due to these facts and the immense number of variables, what you create is your own responsibility.

Remember, changes to improve the trailer's towability may decrease the tow vehicle's performance or put extra strain on the trailer's structure. *TRAILERS — How to Buy & Evaluate* discusses some of these aspects. *Volume 2* and *3* look more closely at concepts and describe calculations one might want to perform to gain insight into these areas while designing a trailer. Any newly built trailer should be checked out and road tested slowly and carefully, preferably in some remote unoccupied area, such as an empty parking lot or test track designed for such maneuvers. An extra wide EMPTY boulevard as one might find at 6am Sunday morning may be more accessible. Freeways, city boulevards and winding mountain roads are least desirable and not recommended. As you venture forth, listen and watch for sounds and sights of trouble. Be sensitive to the movements of the trailer and don't risk anything. Remember that instability can be initiated by downhill grades, wind gusts or passing trucks (to name a few) and caution is the watchword here. Speeds must increase slowly, and any hints of instability heeded and checked immediately and thoroughly. Please don't just keep driving in hopes it will just disappear. An inherently unstable trailer may not show its colors until it's too late. If available, the use of test equipment can improve your perceptions and knowledge.

Because your ability, along with the resulting combinations, modifications, materials and methods used are beyond our control, naturally we cannot assume any responsibility as to the results obtainable. Bear in mind that building a trailer for use on public roads is serious business, as are any vehicle modifications you may attempt. And while few laws exist as restrictions to your design choices, common sense and an accurate assessment of your abilities is imperative to assure your safety.

CHAPTER 1.

DEVELOPING A DESIGN

A. Steps to Organization & Success
    1. State the problem
    2. Lay out the basics
    3. Investigate the options

B. The Successful Trailer
    4. Selecting materials
    5. Selecting components
    6. Calculate sizes & decide configurations

C. Putting It All on Paper.
    7. Select scale and drawing size
    8. Decide final overall dimensions

Designing and building your very own trailer can be fun and very rewarding. To embark on such a project, work through the myriad and numerous questions that inevitably occur and end up with something that will haul whatever bounty you have is worth more than just a pat on the back. But beware . . . this project is fraught with pitfalls and actually carries the potential for creating a lethal weapon. Yes, if your home-built trailer is constructed poorly, it and your tow-car could be so unstable at certain speeds as to become a life threatening risk—one you cannot control. The information in this book and its **Volume 3** will provide many of the keys to avoid such a disaster. **TRAILERS—How to Buy & Evaluate** also contains a simplified summary in the event **Volume 3** is not yet available.

Yes, trailers can be built and hooked to a tow vehicle that are a delight to tow. These trailers don't just fall together by accident. They are tediously and carefully planned using the principles of structures, dynamics and basic engineering laws. In addition, components are selected to be appropriate and optimum for the job.

Don't underestimate the size of this task . . . or the impending responsibility of building something that will not risk your own life or the lives of others. Don't assume your Motor Vehicle or Police Department will check out your trailer for design, towability and safety. They are not engineers. They are there to enforce the laws, not provide you with design expertise. All you can count on your Motor Vehicle Department to do is verify that what you've built is indeed a trailer—not an auto or a truck or a bus—and assign a serial number to it. They also will check for lights and their correct placement, as well as add a serial number to your frame. After you have studied this book and understand its contents, you will know so much more about constructing a trailer that you may well be able to tell them how to build one. However, I don't suggest you do that.

This book is a record of my experience. It has information in it which can possibly be of help to you. It can guide you through the inevitable challenges and be an excellent reference book, there to answer questions when needed. Designing something can be a lot of fun, especially if you have the energy, enthusiasm and focused will-power to carry through the construction and end up with something useful, something you understand stem to stern because you've taken the effort to study the physical laws that affect its performance.

A. STEPS TO ORGANIZATION & SUCCESS

The first step in any project is to PLAN with a capital **P-L-A-N**! This may seem boring and unnecessary, especially when you can just walk to your shop or garage and start welding something together. Welding it together first and planning as you go locks you into something you may find later isn't appropriate. Use a piece of paper to start your building . . . and we'll show you how easy it is to correct your mistakes before they're cast in concrete . . . or steel, as the case may be. If you want to make a change just get out your eraser . . . or a clean sheet of paper. By the way, spouses tend to like the economies of this method, too.

As you draw, you will find groups of questions popping up that need to be worked through before you can finish drawing something. The correct design approach involves a whole series of "oh no, not again" . . . and "what do I do now?" This confusion can be terribly unsettling. But the success of the final product depends on your perseverance in thinking these things through. It may appear to be a lot more effort than the actual building. But that is only because there are so many questions that require brain-work and maybe foot-work to answer. If you follow a standardized procedure in answering your questions you can check off the steps as you go and it will seem a lot easier. Let's look at these steps in detail so you know what to expect and have a pattern to follow.

The process for designing a trailer is the same as for designing anything else. It involves a step by step sequence which leads to an end product. Each step can be rather involved and take a lot of time. But please don't despair. Properly attended to, each step will lead to the next and may answer questions you'll have further downstream. Before you know it everything will fall together and you'll be at your last step. The steps to guide you to success are as follows:

1. State the problem (basic requirements for the trailer);
2. Lay out the basic product using only general, basic dimensions;
3. Investigate thoroughly the options available;
4. Calculate material sizes and overall configuration;
5. Select materials using calculated answers as a guide;
6. Decide on final dimensions to be used;
7. Investigate & select all components;
8. Determine relative positions of all parts and pieces;
9. Lay out the final design using chosen parts and pieces;
10. Transfer all info to the final layout.

These steps are not necessarily done in this order, although it is the order in which you will first encounter the steps. New information obtained in any one step may modify a decision you have already made and cause you to rework a previous step. This checking, changing and rework gives you the ultimate design. It is important to let this process occur; don't allow yourself to become impatient or say "I've already done this." Do it again and again until it is as perfect as you can get it.

It's all done on paper with a pencil, a few straight edges, triangles and lots of erasers. Some of these useful tools are pictured in Figure 1.1. These are the same ones you may have used in high school drafting class. Hauling out that old high school equipment will bring back some memories

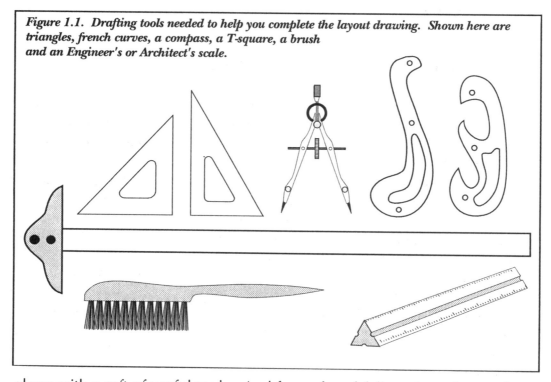

Figure 1.1. Drafting tools needed to help you complete the layout drawing. Shown here are triangles, french curves, a compass, a T-square, a brush and an Engineer's or Architect's scale.

along with a raft of useful tools. And for us frugal folks using what we have can be a financial boon.

Tools in the form of tables, equations and methods are also necessary. *Volume 2* discusses this aspect of design. Used in conjunction with your drafting tools, they give you what it takes to put a trailer design together. All it costs is time—no investment in metal before you're ready. A few chapters into this book, the whole process will be more familiar and comfortable and the steps will fall into place.

Setting goals is another useful tool for moving your project forward. Although your overall goal is to build the trailer, setting your first goal at some intermediate point will minimize discouragement. In fact, if the overall goal to build a trailer is your focus, the importance of a drawing can be easily underestimated—sometimes enough to cause you to completely ignore it. After the drawing is done, though, your next goal can be to spec-out all the required materials; next to buy the materials . . . and so forth.

Doing it step by step in this manner is much more approachable than looking to the overall completion of a hand-built trailer.

As you read through this series of books, **Volume 1, 2** and **3**, many of the complex technical terms you need to understand the trailer, the tow-car and the combination vehicle (trailer and tow-car together) are defined and explained. Use the steps to simplify your project, to give you a guide-line and help you make decisions before you cut metal. The steps will help you in building any project. As you read through this and the next few chapters, continually refer back to the original outline to keep you on track.

STEP 1. State the Problem . . . or Define the Project

The problem statement is very important. It gives the basis from which to launch your whole project and defines the performance requirements for the finished project. Engineers often refer to this step as completing "half the battle". Once a problem, or project, can be defined, it can be clarified and worked through. A trailer that dangles as an idea in your imagination can never be manifested into something useful.

So how do we turn our "ideas" into a problem statement? Start by putting your thoughts on paper—whatever those thoughts are. This doesn't mean talking about them with all your buddies—that can waste precious energy. It means getting out a pad of paper and starting to write. If you enjoy the pad, paper and pencil you're using you'll be able to sit in one place long enough to really think things out. Having the correct drawing or writing tools will turn those "ideas" into something real on paper. Writing things down provides a starting point for organization. Some thoughts you might include regarding your trailer are:

1. Cargo dimensions & weight;
2. Tow vehicle size & specifications, horsepower, wheelbase, rear overhang;
3. A list of places you might take your trailer;
4. The miles you intend to tow your trailer;
5. A list of tasks your trailer may be called upon to perform;
6. Some sketches of what you think might work;
7. The storage space available for your trailer.

From these . . . and a few more facts, you can put together what is called "A Problem Statement" which in reality is a definition of your project. The word "problem" is used because it's what we used in school and it tends to put you in the right frame of mind to analyze all aspects and options. This problem statement might include the trailer's primary use, its auxiliary use and whether it is to be light weight to save gas or extra heavy duty to withstand abuse. Below is an example statement

Sample Problem — Hauling boxes.

1. Primary use—hauling boxes filled with books
2. Cargo weight: 24 boxes @ 60-lbs each = 1440-lbs.
3. Cargo dimensions: each box is 12"x 17"x 36" high
4. Distance travelled: 30 miles x 2 trips per week
   = 60 miles/week = 6240 miles/year.
5. Trailer doesn't need a cover in sunny weather but provisions for a canvas cover would be nice.
6. Trailer cannot weigh more than 550 pounds since the tow vehicle specifications recommend a maximum trailer weight of 2000 pounds.
7. Want to be able to use the trailer on week-ends for recreation—this will increase the mileage by about 5000 miles/year.

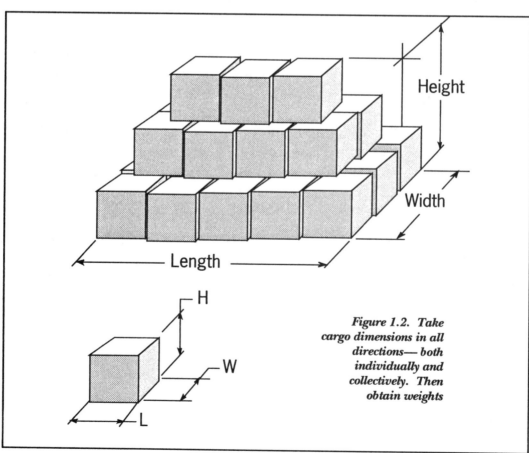

Figure 1.2. Take cargo dimensions in all directions— both individually and collectively. Then obtain weights

STEP 2. Lay Out the Basics

A picture is worth a 1000 words. And getting your trailer from your imagination onto a piece of paper can quickly tell you whether you are envisioning something workable. Although this step calls for only a "rough" sketch, it may not seem so rough if you are unaccustomed to "sketching" things to scale. And yes, it should be done on grided paper to some small scale so that it will fit on an 8-1/2-in x 11-in sheet of paper. This size makes it easier to file the drawing and slip it under the spring of a clip board. Using a clipboard has an ulterior motive because it means you can take it with you to relax in a big soft chair. In this way getting the drawing onto paper becomes relatively painless. Of course, if you're a diehard for straight back chairs and rigidity inspires you, use a desk and a nice large sheet of paper.

If the trailer is really big, though, two letter size sheets could also be used to produce a drawing 11-in x 17-in. A more detailed description of your options in the realm of scales is shown in Figures 1.3 and 1.4 on the next two pages. Following that, on pages 10 and 11, is a background grid, reproduced as Figure 1.5 of this book. Use this if other sources seem to leave you empty handed. Copy this grid onto an 8-1/2 x 11 sheet of paper, it will give you something to start with. Next select an appropriate scale from Figures 1.3 and 1.4.

Plan and position top, side, front and rear views. These can be done freehand by tracing over the grid lines, or you can use a straight edge (triangle or ruler). Use the grid line to count the squares and check your dimensions. Sketching the cargo prior to delineation of your trailer will help verify the correctness of your dimensions and give you something to "wrap" your trailer around. Sketches of the cargo should be on a separate sheet of paper but of the same scale as the trailer drawing.

Figure 1.6 is an example of a rough freehand sketch. If you have drawn the item to scale, the dimensions are not necessary but you may want to include them for reference. Once you have recorded a general idea of your proposed trailer, set it aside for the time being and move onto the next step. The details for your trailer will begin to fall into place as you gather more information.

Figure 1.5 (pg 10 & 11). The grid on pages 10 and 11 is designed to copy and use for layout paper if no other option is available. A division of 5:1 is used. Any of the proportions and scales shown in Figures 1.3 and 1.4 will work with this grid.

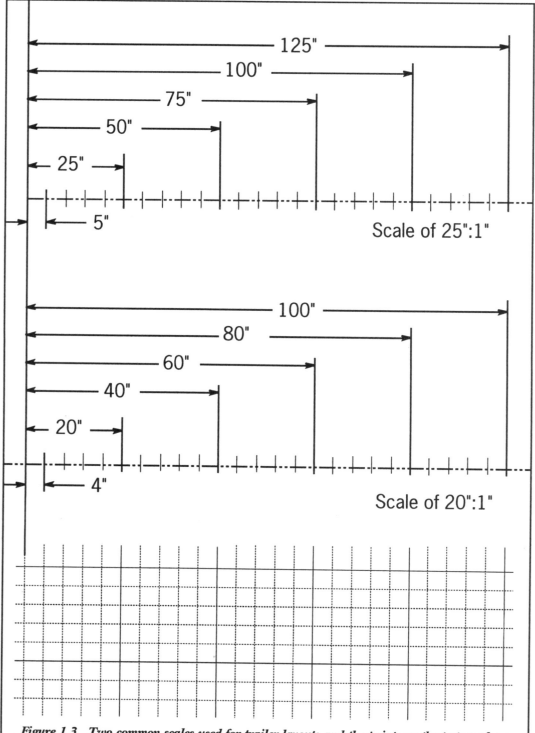

Figure 1.3. Two common scales used for trailer layouts and the points on the paper where the various dimensions fall. A scale of 25:1 will handle 125" on a 5" length: whereas a scale of 20:1 will handle only 100" on a 5" length. The planned length of your trailer will help you decide which scale is most appropriate for your project.

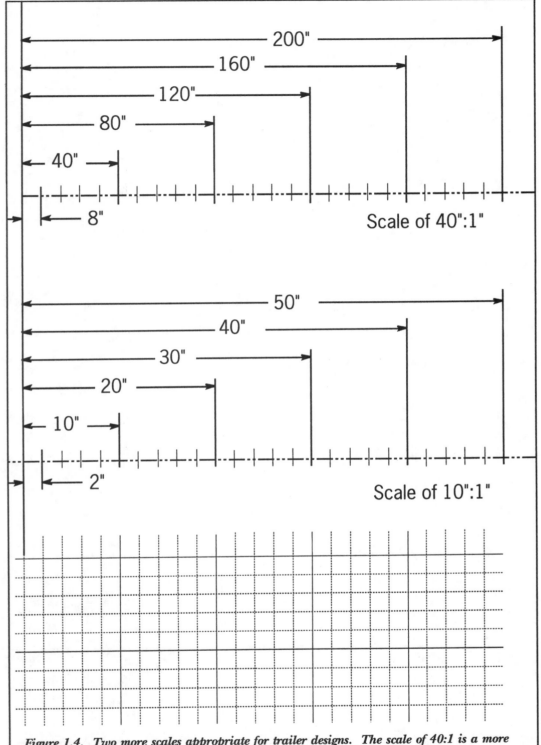

Figure 1.4. *Two more scales appropriate for trailer designs. The scale of 40:1 is a more likely candidate for large trailers and rough layout drawings. The scale of 10:1 works well for small trailers and for preliminary layouts.*

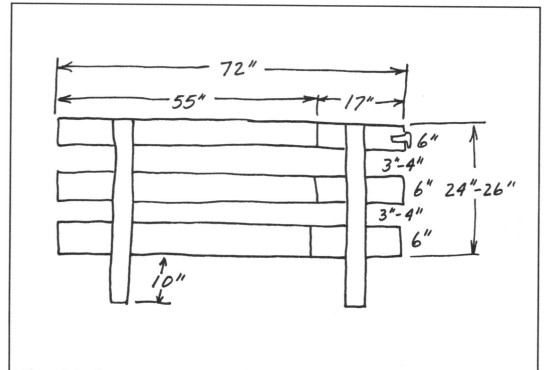

Figure 1.6. A rough freehand sketch of a stake-rack is shown here. Subsequently a detailed drawing was done with more exacting lines and dimensions.

STEP 3. Investigate the Options

Choices, choices everywhere, but what's the one to choose . . . and this is no understatement. The variables and combinations are infinite. This phase of your project could indeed be your most consuming time-wise. It involves gathering as much information about trailers as you can. Facts, figures, numbers and prices are all part of this step. Some of the facts you might include have been discussed in **TRAILERS—How to Buy & Evaluate**, as part of the process of determining what trailer to purchase.

Prepare a folder or envelope for storage of brochures or catalogs. If the folder gets too big, create two or three new to replace the one. Or start a binder with tabs for categories such as suspension, materials, accessories and anything else that seems relevant to you. Keep separate note papers within each tab for such things as notes from phone calls. When you call the same place again it will provide a nice reference record.

When you call potential suppliers, don't be afraid to ask as many questions as necessary to understand the product you intend to purchase. Dimensions, capacity, materials and configuration are areas where

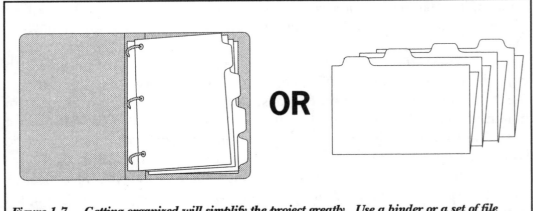

Figure 1.7. Getting organized will simplify the project greatly. Use a binder or a set of file folders. It will start out small and increase in size as you investigate more.

questions are most appropriate. Hopefully this book will have certain answers for you, so your phone calls can be much shorter.

Photographs can also be very helpful. A collection of trailer pictures that look like what you might want to build can help you visualize your end product. Anything to facilitate a clearer view will make the task at hand easier. Learn everything you can about trailers and avoid becoming locked into any particular design or feature before you examine the pros and cons of each one. In other words, keep an open mind at this point and don't rule anything out yet. You may be led to an even better option than your first idea for your final configuration.

B. THE SUCCESSFUL TRAILER

A trailer is considered successful if it carries the load intended, is strong enough, tows easily without sway, loads easily and even disappears while it is not being used only to re-appear when required again. The last attribute is beyond what I know. But the first ones are subjects addressed in the volumes of this book. Designing a trailer basically involves the selection of materials and components and arranging them into a config-uration to fit the requirements of your design as closely as possible.

STEP 4. Selecting Materials

Materials are a major part of your project. Leave lots of time for studies in this area. Understanding the advantages and disadvantages of differing materials and the properties associated with varying shapes is an integral part of this material selection process. Figure 1.8 illustrates cross sections of material commonly used on trailers along with a few not so common shapes. Shown are some of the choices you have for framework materials.

Basic and generalized ideas of materials are something worth considering before you begin drawing. You may already know that steel is best for the frame and wood is best for the floor; but, an aluminum diamond plate may also sound pretty good. However, if aluminum is not available to you, (either physically or financially) your choice may still be wood. Whatever you select, just be sure the material is right for the job.

Calculations can help with knowing if the material you've chosen is strong enough. **Volume 2** discusses calculations used for choosing an optimum shape for a given load and elaborates on properties important to understand. Your final choice is generally a co-ordination of requirements, such as load pick-up points, cargo dimensions, strength and connection methods. Be prepared to use different size or different gauge materials in different places throughout the trailer. For instance, fenders do not require the mass of material the axle requires. Building a trailer from one size such

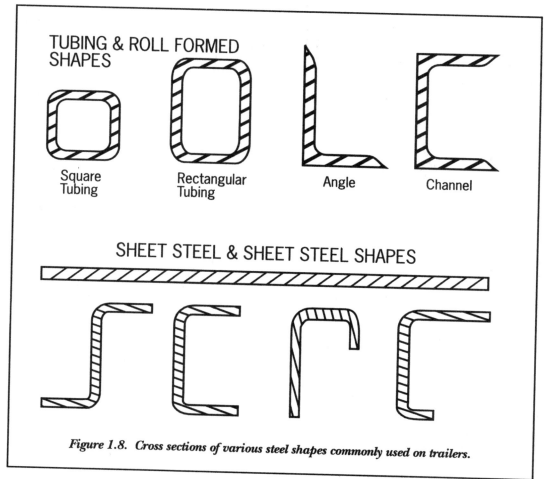

Figure 1.8. Cross sections of various steel shapes commonly used on trailers.

material is apt to produce undesirable results. Using material big enough to carry the load without overdoing it is efficient weight wise and can even be better space wise. While this approach may appear obvious to some, the concept of variable sizing is important to understand.

Scrap steel narrows the options and may force a result you didn't desire. Building with "what's good and heavy" also adds weight fast and a trailer too massive may result; thus imprecise approaches are often detrimental.

The materials from which a trailer is made determine its entire character. And although the selection process can seem tedious and exhausting, you will be well rewarded for your patience and careful selection of each piece.

STEP 5. *Selecting Components*

Selecting the axles, hubs, springs, fenders and coupler is not all there is to building a trailer—although it is a major part . . . and lots of trailer projects are started with the visualization of just these parts. These and several other individual components combine with raw steel, wood and/or aluminum of the frame to round out your trailer and bring it to a complete product. To be sure your system is adequate and appropriate, each component must be thoroughly investigated. This includes the determination of capacities, sizes, dimensions, fit with adjacent parts and appropriateness for its duty. Chapter 3, 4 and 5 of this Volume describe most of the components you need to complete the trailer and provide guidelines for their selection. With the guidance in these chapters, supplier's catalogs will make a lot more sense and you'll be able to ask more knowledgeable questions.

Many trailer components require expensive specialized equipment to

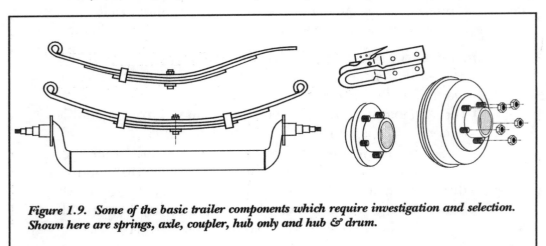

Figure 1.9. Some of the basic trailer components which require investigation and selection. Shown here are springs, axle, coupler, hub only and hub & drum.

manufacture. For small quantities of trailers—like one only—an outright purchase from someone who has already invested the time and money in equipment is the easiest solution. Items such as hubs, couplers, axles, wheels and spindles obviously fall into this category. Even less major specialized accessories for design improvements—such as jacks, fenders, tie down hardware, tongue stiffeners, *Step Neck*™ and light brackets—can be added to this list of better or certainly easier to purchase components outright. In many instances these products provide much better solutions than you are likely to devise yourself. You may find that because of cost or maybe even, "I'd just rather do it myself," you'll be tempted to fabricate your own parts or components. Just beware! The design and fabrication effort may be more than you bargained for. A few major components are shown in Figure 1.9.

STEP 6. Calculate Sizes & Decide Configurations.

A trailer's final configuration and ultimate strength depends on the materials used and their placement in the overall scheme of things. Calculations can be instrumental in selecting the optimum material placement and designing the final configuration.

Trailer calculations, fall into 2 major groups: 1) those used to determine material (and trailer) strength and 2) those which determine a trailer's dynamic stability while moving down the road. Both help to define the overall configuration. The objective of calculations as discussed in *Volume 2*, is to arrive at a design which is strong enough and stable enough to handle the required loads with adequate safety margin, while at the same time avoiding excess strength and the associated weight, cost and potential contribution to instability.

While strength calculations are fairly basic, many trials and errors may be required. The components of such a calculation include variables which represent three important aspects—material, shape and load.

1) The variable representing the **material** is called the *allowable tensile stress* which is a reduced percentage of the material's tensile strength.
2) The variable for the cross sectional **shape** of the material is either *area* or a value called *moment of inertia*.
3) The variable for the **load** configuration is called *bending moment* and/or *shear load*. For continuous loads such as dirt or hay, the values are quite different than for loads concentrated in one or two places as you would have with an auto, a horse or a piece of equipment.

By combining two of these variables, it is possible to obtain the third. Thus with items 1 and 3 known, the minimum required *moment of inertia* can be derived. This is an important capability since load and material stress are often known and material size is in question. Once the safety factor is considered, included and the moment of inertia is calculated, tables can be consulted to select a beam of optimum strength and size to easily support the load in question. Many reference books are available where properties and values for different shaped cross sections are cataloged by material size. The Appendix of **Volume 2** includes such a table with an extensive listing of materials commonly used in trailer building. Sometimes knowing the strength of an existing piece of material is necessary. By first obtaining the moment of inertia from tables, using the known adjusted tensile stress, the allowable load can then be computed.

Suppliers can be found for a myriad of materials—steel, bar and rod, steel tube, steel sheet, aluminum, magnesium, fiberglass, etc. But few, if any, can tell you the actual strength of the materials when used as you will use them. Fortunately these suppliers can and are usually happy to provide you with the *tensile* or *ultimate stress* of the material. However, the actual carrying strength of the product as configured by you is a computed number . . . one you will have to determine yourself.

Calculations to assess dynamic stability and performance are two-fold. One approach uses a formula to obtain the damping ratio at a particular speed. Damping ratio is a number which gives an indication of a trailer's ability to return to straight line towing after some disturbance. Damping ratio also predicts the speed at which the trailer, because of its configuration, components and/or loading is apt to become unstable and begin to sway. Reducing a trailer's tendency to sway is an important consideration since 90% of trailer accidents reported are preceded by trailer sway. And stories from friends and acquaintances abound of the terror (and worse) suffered by those caught in the throes of a whipping trailer.

In addition, the position of a trailer's center of gravity can aggravate or enhance body roll and stability especially in emergency situations. A trailer that can slide sideways and not overturn gives a driver a much better chance of staying out of serious trouble. Calculations for overturn stability and damping ratio are used to predict this behavior. **Volume 3** covers these two subjects which can be most useful in helping you create a trailer that will react mildly, if at all, to disturbances you encounter.

C. PUTTING IT ALL ON PAPER

Now you're ready for the layout drawing: the keeper and recorder of all your work. Actually this is the most exciting part of planning your trailer . . . especially if you've convinced yourself to take your time and do it slowly. This drawing is the ledger of your whole design. All information you concoct or deduce is in some manner eventually recorded on this piece of paper. The six previous steps to organization and success include information that is transferred to this drawing. Laid out to scale, this drawing shows every frame member, suspension part and accessory in its proper and relative position. It has a top view, a side view and probably several end or cross sectional views. The information for this drawing is garnered from calculations, research and shopping and includes cargo dimensions, material sizes, component shapes and dimensions determined from calculations.

Combining this myriad of materials is easily done graphically if each item is drawn to scale, all on separate pieces of paper. The drawings can then be brought together by tracing the separate sketches onto a complete layout drawing. For future changes or additions, the separate drawings provide a good reference. And by drawing each to scale you will also be forced to find the dimensions you are missing.

A standardized lay out of top, front and side views will produce a drawing with the kind of detail needed. The chapters of this book, along with *Volume 2* (structural considerations) and *Volume 3* (towability considerations), are designed to assist you through the thought processes necessary to produce this drawing. Chapters 3, 4 and 5 of this volume ease the component shopping process, Chapter 2 discusses the overall view of possible creations and their results. Chapter 6 contains suggestions for welding and final assembly of the trailer. *TRAILERS—How to Buy & Evaluate* also provides an excellent laymen's summary of *Volumes 2* and *3*.

STEP 7. Select Scale & Drawing Size

The scale of your drawing is an important consideration for all drawings. You may think this is the most difficult part as you sit there with a blank sheet of paper . . . and maybe even a blank stare . . . wondering where to start. Once you've decided on a scale, realize that you may later need to change it. The choice of scale depends on personal preference and the size paper selected as well as what might be available to you. Scales of 1:10, 1:8, 1:5 or 1:4 are popular choices. If you have no paper to start with, hot foot it on down to your local drafting or art supply store. "Clear Print" brand paper should be available with imprinted light blue lines in divisions of 10 to 1, 8 to 1, 4 to 1, or 5 to 1. These scales, shown in Figure 1.10, are easily adapted to your trailer drawing. The drawing should be large enough to examine the detail, but not so large as to lose sight of the overall concept.

Sometimes its best to start with 10 to 1 or 8 to 1 and draw details double size in 4 to 1 or 5 to 1. Architect's and engineer's scales adjusted to the correct divisor (see Figure 1.1) are also available at drafting and art supply stores. Using these measuring devices makes it much easier to add dimensions together or subtract them, since the divisions read in the scale you've chosen. Continually having to divide 1-inch into 5 pieces detracts from concentration on more important issues.

No matter what scale you use, convert all your dimensions to straight inches (or centimeters). Trying to work with feet and inches requires continual conversions and difficult subtractions and additions. Getting bogged down in number conversions invites mistakes. Tenths and

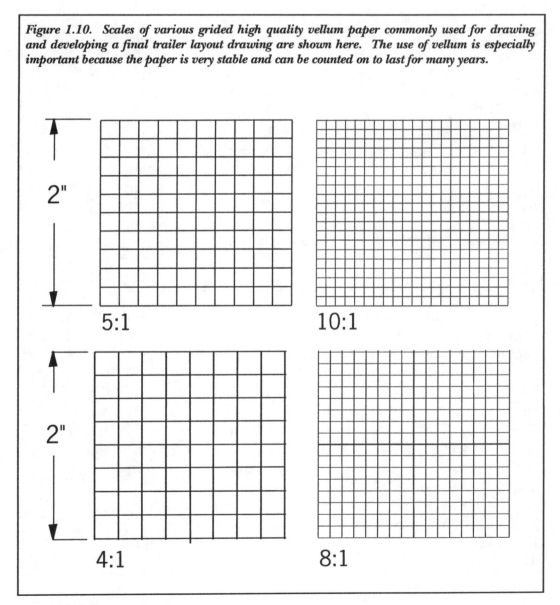

Figure 1.10. Scales of various grided high quality vellum paper commonly used for drawing and developing a final trailer layout drawing are shown here. The use of vellum is especially important because the paper is very stable and can be counted on to last for many years.

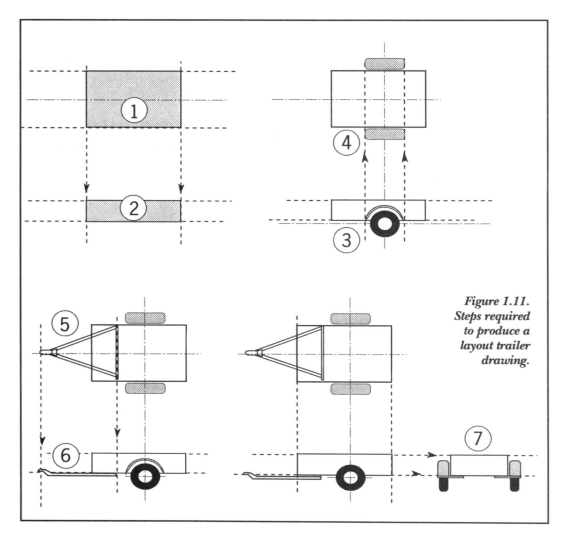

Figure 1.11.
Steps required
to produce a
layout trailer
drawing.

hundredths of an inch are also easier to use than fractions. In addition, calculations are more easily completed using inches and hundredths without conversions. Architects use feet and inches because of custom and because their dimensions are often very long—like 600 feet. At that dimension one inch has much less significance. To add to the confusion, highways are built with feet and tenths of a foot; they, too, have very long dimensions. Trailers are seldom longer than 30-feet overall, which is 360 inches; or 40 feet, which is 480 inches. In fact, most are less than 20 feet. So make it easy on yourself. Convert feet to inches and fractions to 10ths (0.X) and hundredths (0.XX)!

After you have guessed the approximate size for each view and decided on an appropriate scale, the first item to draw is the cargo. This should be done on a separate piece of paper using the same scale as you plan to use on the overall layout of the trailer. Since you will be using the

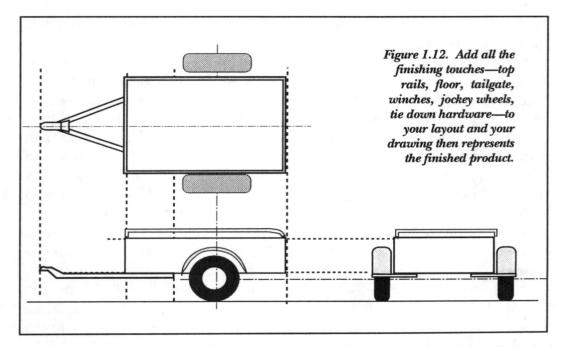

Figure 1.12. Add all the finishing touches—top rails, floor, tailgate, winches, jockey wheels, tie down hardware—to your layout and your drawing then represents the finished product.

cargo drawing as an overlay to check dimensions it is best to use vellum or tracing paper. A side view, top view, front and end view of the cargo should serve your purpose. If you have several items of cargo, draw each one. Be sure to include any unusual protuberances. If at all possible, lay your cargo out on the garage floor and sketch the envelope around it. This will permit a 3D view of the cargo in place. With dimensions and knowledge of the cargo, you have a good idea of the size your trailer needs to be.

STEP 8. Decide Final Overall Dimensions

And now, after drawing the cargo, you can start on the trailer. Again we need a clean sheet of paper with room for a side view, a top view, an end view, a front view, a few sections and perhaps several details. Cut a large enough piece of paper for all views to fit. Roll size drawing paper will probably be wide enough and can be cut to any length. A 22" x 34" or 48" is convenient for a 10 to 1 scale and if you have a drawing table large enough a larger scale with a 30" by 44", 52", or 60" is even better. The paper can always be cut down but adding to its length poses a problem. Check out the paper size before cutting.

With a large sheet of paper now in place, the lines most easily placed first are the top view outside dimensions of the rectangular framework, as shown in Figure 1.11. The side view front and back lines can then be projected downward. Once the side view tire/fender position is drawn it can be projected upward back to the top view. Remember wheels, tires and fenders protrude beyond the basic rectangle in the top view, so leave room. Also dimensions eventually get added to all views and room is needed for this later. Placement of the tongue in the top view can then be projected downward to the side view. Doing a little in one view and then moving to another view to do a little more is more efficient and easier than trying to do all of one view before moving onto the next. Co-ordination of other components—fenders, suspension, lights, accessories —between views will build your drawing to completion. The size of the area required for drawing can grow quickly so keep your lines light to begin with until you have a pretty good idea of the envelope required for drawings and dimensions. Figure 1.12 is the completed drawing before dimensions are added.

It sounds so simple! And it truly can be. Just follow the steps, use this book for reference, gather all the data you can from other sources. Now combine it all into one pot and in a short time you'll be ready to cut metal with the right dimensions and a precise plan.

CHAPTER 2.

OVERALL CONSIDERATIONS

Trailers look very simple and it is hard to imagine anything complex about them. But once you get into the design, you will find a complex menagerie of questions whose answers are not always so easy to find. It is important to understand that questions not answered properly can lead to problems. "He who thought they were simple" and refuses to believe otherwise usually finds an end result of "Its not exactly what I originally planned." The structural horrors that abound in the paddocks of trailer storage areas are testament to this all too common approach. These trailers often lack the strength and integrity to do their intended job. Most are far from works of art and have pretty convincingly grown from after-thought added to after-thought. Performance is also often reflected in their towability . . . or lack thereof.

How to avoid this? You took the first sensible step by buying this book. Hopefully it will push you to gathering information and under-standing as much about trailers as you can. This book is a record of my experience and can add greatly to your file and library. However, it is not the last word so don't eliminate other sources. My experience is that understanding the concepts along with the proper use of certain basic tools, you can build a trailer the right way. It is even possible to reduce or eliminate sway—making your trailer a delight to tow. Your trailer can have an opportunity for unlimited life and pleasant towing. Understanding and respecting the capacity of the myriad of components, materials and concepts required to build any trailer has benefits.

Some important questions one might want to ponder are: What causes trailer sway? How and why does axle placement effect towability? Why is CG important? What difference does a frame make? What do I need to know about trailer tongues? What does capacity really mean? Why is a lower mass (or weight) better? How can my trailer have a lower mass and retain the same strength? Are these questions you have vaguely phrased yourself? Probably so. Answers to some of these questions were discussed in **TRAILERS—How to Buy & Evaluate**. To reproduce that information here in toto would detract from the subject of this book. However, because an in-depth grasp of some of these concepts can effect your end result significantly we will review them briefly and strongly suggest you peruse the *Buy/Evaluate* text. The discussion in this book is also more directed to ideas and concepts required to understand the design and building of the trailer. Your having a working knowledge of the technical aspects of trailer design will improve the design of your trailer and will go a long way to making it a success. This chapter in particular illuminates a few of the most important overall concepts.

A. THE ESSENCE OF CG.

The point from which an item can be lifted with perfect balance is called its *center of gravity*. For example, a formula type race car can often be lifted by its roll bar and remain level as it is carried off the race track by a tow truck (See Figure 2.1). It is being lifted through its horizontal CG. Machinery is often fitted with a loop for lifting with a chain and forklift. As the machine is lifted it will not tilt from side to side. It also is being lifted through its horizontal or lateral center of gravity. Trailers have a CG, too, just like every other physical body. Knowing the position of that CG can help you determine a trailer's suitability for being towed.

Finding the horizontal CG of many items is usually easy. Figure 2.2 demonstrates the weighing of an object to obtain its actual CG. (NOTE: This lifting and weighing must be approached with great caution and safety and should only be attempted by persons with experience in this area.) Weigh each end of the item and calculate the center point as in Figure 2.2. Determining the vertical CG position requires a little more tenacity.   The simplest way is to turn the item on its side and find its balance point in the

*Figure 2.1. A formula car is lifted by its rollbar which is usually built through the vehicle's CG.
Photo courtesy of D.E. Baer, Sunland, Calif.*

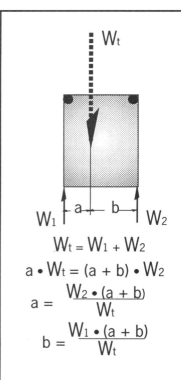

$$W_t = W_1 + W_2$$
$$a \cdot W_t = (a + b) \cdot W_2$$
$$a = \frac{W_2 \cdot (a + b)}{W_t}$$
$$b = \frac{W_1 \cdot (a + b)}{W_t}$$

Figure 2.2. The total weight and the position of a body's CG can be found. Obtain a weight at each corner and calculate as above to obtain the distance to the CG from each side.

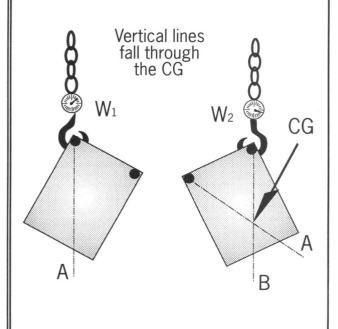

Figure 2.3. Weighing an object to obtain its actual CG can often be quite a task. To do it as shown above, it must be approached with great caution and safety. An object can be lifted from one corner and then the other. If a plumb bob is hung from the lifted corner, the cord will fall through the plane of the CG. The point where the lines connect is the CG.

same manner we did the horizontal CG. Unfortunately, this method is often not too practical. Another way is to lift the item from an upper corner (if angling it is acceptable) with a spring scale attached. This will permit the reading of a weight and provide a vertical line from the lifted corner through the center of weight. This line can be marked on the side of the machine. Do the same with another corner. The intersection of the two lines is the CG—both horizontal and vertical placement. This method is not without risks, though. Damage to you or the equipment—if it should slip—is a real possibility. Please take special precautions and have someone around that knows something about the safety procedures necessary for such a task. Accurate measurements are important and if not obtained, the reliability of the resulting numbers will suffer.

The CG can also be calculated . . . as long as one knows the weight of each piece and the exact locations of the CG of each individual part. This method can be fraught with inaccuracies because of all the little pieces that are too easily missed, such as welds or oil in containers.

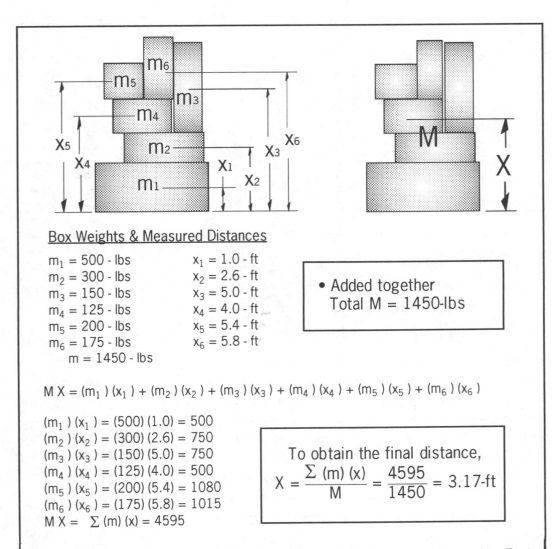

Box Weights & Measured Distances

$m_1 = 500$ - lbs $x_1 = 1.0$ - ft
$m_2 = 300$ - lbs $x_2 = 2.6$ - ft
$m_3 = 150$ - lbs $x_3 = 5.0$ - ft
$m_4 = 125$ - lbs $x_4 = 4.0$ - ft
$m_5 = 200$ - lbs $x_5 = 5.4$ - ft
$m_6 = 175$ - lbs $x_6 = 5.8$ - ft
 $m = 1450$ - lbs

- Added together
  Total M = 1450-lbs

$$M X = (m_1)(x_1) + (m_2)(x_2) + (m_3)(x_3) + (m_4)(x_4) + (m_5)(x_5) + (m_6)(x_6)$$

$(m_1)(x_1) = (500)(1.0) = 500$
$(m_2)(x_2) = (300)(2.6) = 750$
$(m_3)(x_3) = (150)(5.0) = 750$
$(m_4)(x_4) = (125)(4.0) = 500$
$(m_5)(x_5) = (200)(5.4) = 1080$
$(m_6)(x_6) = (175)(5.8) = 1015$
$M X = \Sigma (m)(x) = 4595$

To obtain the final distance,
$$X = \frac{\Sigma (m)(x)}{M} = \frac{4595}{1450} = 3.17\text{-ft}$$

Figure 2.4. Calculation of a center of gravity vertical position for a stack of boxes. A trailer is slightly more complex but is handled the same way by using the weights of individual parts and the distance to their CG's. Volume 3 of this book illustrates this procedure for a trailer.

Knowing or finding the CG of each piece is a tedious task. Each piece has to be measured, calculated and the CG found separately. Figure 2.4 illustrates this method. As you can see, one is left with choosing among a few less than desirable methods and realizing the potential for inaccuracies.

If you are attempting to determine the CG of a trailer that hasn't been built an even greater challenge awaits you. However, if you don't find a way to at least estimate it, the consequences could be dire indeed as can be observed by studying Figures 2.5 through 2.7. Figure 2.5 is a trailer I followed for several city miles. Its body roll caught my eye as it left a supply house dock. Many factors are alarming about this example. The overload is evident from the curve of the axle and camber of the wheels

and tires. In addition, the lowered tail of the tow vehicle suggests an excessive tongue weight. Although this could occur from a load bias toward the front of the trailer, the other factors suggest it to be an overall load excess. In motion, the body roll was severe and aggravated by the body being built over the top of the small tires and the meager T-tongue. I was grateful to observe the trailer did not exceed 35-mph while I was watching.

Talk about high CG's, the trailer in Figure 2.6 has to take the cake. Used around a farm at 5-mph, this trailer would be its dutiful best. Unfortunately, if loaded full on public roads, this little gem could be lethal indeed. We put numbers to this trailer's dimensions in **Volume 3**, where you will see what we mean.

The trailer in Figure 2.7 is another contender for top prize. At least the body fits down between the wheels and the tires are a decent size. The trailer's downfall is first, its loosely constructed wooden body, in addition to its resulting CG position up and over the automotive differential axle in addition to the long soft springs. The spindly unreinforced T-tongue would provide little resistance to instability or sideways swings which are certainly invited by the the short tongue and long springs. Other points of interest are the decorative fenders, one bald tire and the heavy wooden box held with steel banding material (which I found in my own experience breaks very easily with stretching impact loads). I would recommend low speeds, light loads and close-to-home activities for this little number. You see how easy

Figure 2.6. This interesting configuration, showed up at a desert construction site. Thank goodness it's small. Hopefully when loaded, it's towed by a large vehicle.

Not a recommended design.

it is to end up with something less than desirable? If these trailers had been drawn up and laid out on paper first, problems could well have been recognized in advance and results may have been as the trailer shown in Figure 2.8. If dimensions or components need to be modified to position the CG correctly, it is much easier to do so before things are welded in place.

The trailer shown in Figure 2.8 has not only a bed that sits down between the wheels but also short stiff springs, a long tongue and a CG that is low and forward. Ideally towing trailers are designed in a similar manner with the horizontal CG position in front of the axle, the vertical CG only slightly above the wheel centerline and the lateral CG centered. This positioning is shown in Figure 2.9. When these criteria aren't met

Figure 2.7. This trailer speaks for itself. No tongue weight, tail heavy. long springs—several sources of problems. Not a model I'd particularly like to own. How about you?

Not a recommended design.

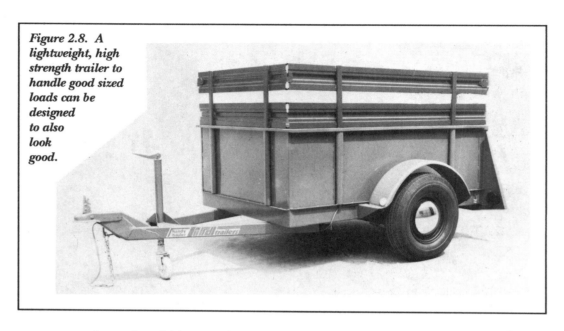

Figure 2.8. A lightweight, high strength trailer to handle good sized loads can be designed to also look good.

compensations should be made in other factors. The factors on a trailer that effect the CG location are numerous. A few are listed here:

wheel and tire height; axle drop and square size; spring hanger design and its attachment to the frame; spring mounting to axle (above or below); type of spring used—slipper, standard, torsion; frame materials used—height and relative position; tongue-to-frame and coupler-to-tongue attachment.

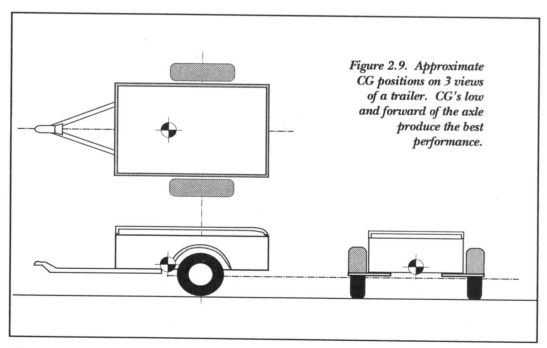

Figure 2.9. Approximate CG positions on 3 views of a trailer. CG's low and forward of the axle produce the best performance.

These factors can and should be manipulated to make the trailer's CG acceptable. Generally, the lower the CG, the more apt you are to develop a trailer with towing stability. However, trailers with higher CG's can be built with towing stability if other factors—tongue length, rear overhang, suspension —are adjusted to compensate. Arriving at the right position for the CG in relation to all components and requirements for the trailer is of vital importance. Further guidelines to finding the optimum placement for center of gravity are provided in *Volume 3*.

B. TRAILER STRUCTURE

The trailer's framework and structure is its backbone and the skeleton to which all parts are attached. It determines ultimate strength and useability. Its configuration can vary extensively and will be greatly affected by the materials used. The framework will determine the trailer's ability to carry your cargo. Indeed, you must admit, an attempt to carry a boat on a horse trailer would be pretty ridiculous, and vice-versa even worse. Besides pure useability, design will have a great effect on the trailer's stability, in addition to its suitability for use with your tow vehicle. No wonder the framework design is so important. If done properly, framework design is one of the most difficult steps to complete.

As many seem to think, a trailer is NOT just an axle, wheels, tires and a coupler. It is a complex conglomeration of many different material shapes and sizes, a myriad of odd and unusual parts including the more obvious just mentioned ones. Suspensions alone can contain over 25 different types of parts, and well over 100 parts all summed up for the whole trailer. Frameworks suffer no simpler agglomerations with main rails, cross members, tongue pieces, braces, brackets, lights, accessories and so forth. Much study, work and thought are required to co-ordinate the construction of such a complex assemblage of parts; that is, if you want to do it right. Manufacturers in the business face almost insurmountable inventory problems especially if customized designs are offered. The trailer design task along with the need for planning certainly should not be underestimated.

What parts of the trailer are considered to be the framework? The tongue, the longitudinal members, the cross-braces and sometimes the bed, although the bed may often just sit on top. In a covered trailer, the members supporting the walls and roof are also considered framework. Deciding what materials to use for each of these parts can be quite a chore. The material has to be strong enough, but too strong quickly makes a trailer too heavy; thus it has to be light enough. The shape has to be right and correctly positioned for the load bearing on it. Questions one might ask are: Is it low enough, wide enough, high enough? Does it need sides? What kind of cross-bracing? Where to place the cross-bracing? How should the tongue be constructed? Where to store the loading ramps or the tailgate, if any? Fitting these and a mile long list of other requirements into one trailer is the challenge of designing and creating the ultimate.

Cargo position, material, capacity and end use must be considered simultaneously when laying the groundwork. This sounds like a tall order and can be overwhelming. The trick is to look at one part at a time then the next, then the next. When each individual area seems to make sense, compare and combine them.

Some people refuse to do this preliminary work because it is just too involved. Others don't even realize that it should be done. Results for these people are often very different than expected. After years of waiting to have time to do it, a friend of mine built a trailer he considered to be the ultimate. He designed it for a gross of 5000-lbs because he wanted to carry about 3500-lbs. He used the best and strongest tubing he could find. He laid it out on his garage floor and assembled it as he went. He wanted to be sure the trailer was plenty strong and would take a beating. When the Motor Vehicle Department required a certified weight on the trailer, he was aghast to find the trailer all by itself weighed 4000-lbs. Don't laugh! This is not a difficult thing to do. It happens all the time to almost every project where planning, drawings and calculations are not part of the process. With a drawing and weight calcs in advance, this could have been predicted and even prevented. With a drawing, weight can be saved or added as required.

Poorly planned and under performing trailers are easy to find. Figure 2.10 is such an example. This trailer obviously grew from spare pieces of steel and an initial angle framework . . . as many do. My guess is that when the small angle and large flat surface were tested with the desired load, it didn't work too well. So the front cross-brace and side truss were added along with the doubled tongue. The tongue is built up in the vertical direction but lacks horizontal reinforcement. Although the trusses along the side work well to reduce front and rear drooping, the lack of suspension will accelerate fatigue, especially in a trailer with such fragile connections. Hopefully the bar at the rear is not used to tie anything of significance; its anchoring is far from adequate for even a small load applied at the top. (Notice that the left side is already angled forward.) Figure 2.11 is a lightweight car trailer used for the same purpose. It is strong in the areas where strength is required. Even years of wear and tear have failed to create the eyesore of Figure 2.10.

Talk about massive frames. The one in Figure 2.12 is indeed that.

Figure 2.10. Various views of a trailer with questionable destiny parked by the roadside. Do you get the impression this trailer was constructed of scrap metal?

Not a recommended design.

Figure 2.11.
An IRD trailer
with it's long tongue
and step up coupler, in
addition to years of wear and tear.

Except for the weathered wood, the frame rails actually appear to be quite light for what they'll carry and the machine bent tongue is actually stronger than most. The wheels and tires appear to be massive enough to handle the load it was designed for. On the other hand, a trailer of this size should have a tubing tongue or the channel should be made into tubing. For towability, I would like to see a longer tongue, especially in light of the higher CG. And a coupler certainly needs to be added. To think of towing even the weight of the trailer with a single pin of 3/4" to 1" diameter is beyond my comprehension. All in all, for a heavy duty trailer, this one looks grubby but structurally is much better than most. If I were in the market for such a trailer, I would purchase it and make the few minor changes to upgrade it with a lunette eye, coupler, fenders and lights as well as repair or replace the wooden bed. It is difficult to tell if suspension exists. If not, this is a definite drawback and may well temper my decision.

Other massive frameworks can generally be found on trailers constructed for the government as shown in Figure 2.13. The size of the bed (5-ft x 8-ft) is small relative to the beefy structure. The heaviest cargo is probably dirt or mud, although the gravel currently in the trailer is no light weight. The most severe survival test, however, is the ability to be dropped unscathed from a helicopter. The suspension, wheels and tires are probably far larger than required for most of its functions, but with a free-fall of any distance, something pretty massive is needed. These trailers are very costly

Figure 2.12 A neglected, but basically structurally sound, heavy duty number sits with a For Sale sign, awaiting a new owner.

to build and result in a great expense for the government. I'm certainly not recommending all trailers be built in this manner, however, something can be learned from this one.

While we're talking about large trailers, check out the one in Figure 2.14 and compare it with 2.13. In spite of the diagonal tension bars along the sides, the frame still sags at either end. It is hard to believe that cardboard could be so heavy to create the wear and tear this trailer seems to be experiencing—but indeed it can. Cardboard is definitely not light.

Figure 2.13. A typical government style, extra heavy duty trailer is loaded with gravel. How much does it weigh? Estimate the load by multiplying the volume times the density of gravel.
Density of dry, loose gravel varies from 90-105-lbs/ft³.
With a volume = 5' x 8' x 1.5' = 60-ft³, the weight of the gravel is 5400-6300-lbs.
With a trailer weight of 1200-lbs the whole rig could easily weigh more than 6600-lbs.

Figure 2.14. This trailer was found to be towed by a one or two ton truck. After computing the weight of the trailer and cargo it needs at least that. I estimated the overall dimensions of the trailer bed to be 24-feet long, 6-1/2-ft high and 8-ft wide. Assuming the load of corrugated cardboard on top would fill the cracks in the bottom area (this is conservative), the total volume of cardboard would be

$$24' \times 6' \times 8' = 1152\text{-ft}^3.$$

Corrugated densities range from 6#/ft^3 to 20#/ft^3 according to people in the industry.

A popular 200# test single wall corrugated material weighs 9.6 to 12#/ft^3.

At 9.6 #/ft^3, this cardboard cargo weighs **11,059-lbs.**

At 12#/ft^3, still a conservative estimate, it weighs a whopping **13,824-lbs.**

And if it is extra heavy duty cardboard, it will weigh 20#/ft^3 = **23,040-lbs.**

vs

Allowable trailer capacity with existing axles = **7000-lbs** total

Wow! That' a lot of cardboard.
You thought this trailer looked overloaded. Guess what? It is!

(The next question one has to ask, "How do trailers like this get licensed?")

After weighing a small stack of folded cardboard boxes and computing the density to be about 9-lb/ft^3, I then checked with a local manufacturer and verified my measurements. By measuring the wheels and scaling the rest of the photo, I calculated the weight of cardboard to be in excess of 10,000-lbs as discussed in Figure 2.14. I bet the owners think their load is much less and they never sat down to really figure it out. In addition, a 24-foot trailer made of channel would have to weigh at least 2500-lbs and maybe even 3500-lbs. The wheels and tires certainly aren't a style to have a capacity of more than 1800-lbs each, nor will they fit axles of more than 3500-lb capacity. Thus the gross capacity on this trailer computes out to be 7000-lbs in round figures. Yet the cargo and trailer together weigh more than 11,000-lbs (a 50% overload) or 14,000-lbs (a 100% overload).

This story is not so uncommon. The hay trailer in Figure 2.15 is

Determine total weight by using density found
from measured dimensions and weight.
Each bale weighs 100 to 135-lbs.
Volume of each bale = 1.33-ft x 1.67-ft x 3.5-ft = 7.8-ft^3

Total quantity of bales = 157

Approximate
dimensions for
a bale of hay
or straw

16" =
1.33-ft

20" =
1.67-ft

42" = 3.5-ft

A. Determine weight using density.

Density, then is approximately = $\dfrac{110\text{-lbs}}{7.8\text{-ft}^3}$ = 14-lbs/ft^3

Thus, minimum total volume of hay =
210" x 120" x 84" = 2,116,000-in^3 =

$$\frac{2,116,000\text{-in}^3}{1728\,\text{in}^3/\text{ft}^3} = 1225\ \text{ft}^3$$

1225-ft^3 @ 14-lbs/ft^3 = 17,150-lbs

B. Determine weight by counting the bales

and multiplying by the weight of each bale.
Each bale weighs 100 to 135-lbs as weighed.
Estimates and guesses, though, range from 80 to 120-lbs for different bales.
157 bales @ 40-lbs each = 6,280-lbs = Estimated Weight
157 bales @ 100-lbs each = 15,700-lbs
157 bales @ 135-lbs each = 21,195-lbs

Figure 2.15. Overloaded hay trailers show up frequently in farming communities. Fortunately their speeds are usually slow. This trailer is loaded to the gills with alfalfa hay, which turns out to be quite heavy. Its weight easily falls between 15,000 and 20,000-lbs. That's a sizable load for a trailer rated at 10,000-lbs—certainly not a match I would recommend at any speed.

another example of overloading, although the percent overload is not as great. The weight of the hay calculates out to weigh about 14,000-lbs. This wouldn't be so bad if the trailer had three axles and the tow truck was at least a one ton model. But the axles are a 5200-lb mobile home style and there are only two of them. The truck appears to be a 3/4-ton model. Hopefully the chosen journey is short and slow and on smooth roads. On another outing, I followed a similar truck and a load and believe it or not, a similar amount of hay was carried on an even less adequate trailer more like the one in Figure 2.14.

The car trailer of Figure 2.16 is rated to carry 5000-lbs. Its total weight is about 1500-lbs, even with the tool box. For a 7000-lb gross, a payload of 5500-lbs can be handled. But the wheels and tires don't come large enough, so the top capacity is actually 6800-lbs less 1500-lbs, for a net load of 5300-lbs. These kinds of calculations need to be run through for each combination of loading and trailer pair. The trick to keeping weight under control is to use material as light as possible (using calculations as a guide) and reinforce in highly stressed areas, but reinforce smoothly. Notice the tongue stiffeners where the tongue attaches to the front cross member. Similar reinforcements are used extensively under the trailer.

To understand this a little more, study the mobile home frame of Figure 2.17. Before a house is added, these frames are very floppy for their weight. A slight twist is even visible in the picture if studied carefully. A larger twist is possible by stepping on one corner. These are not good frames to make into flatbeds because they are heavy and inefficient. They

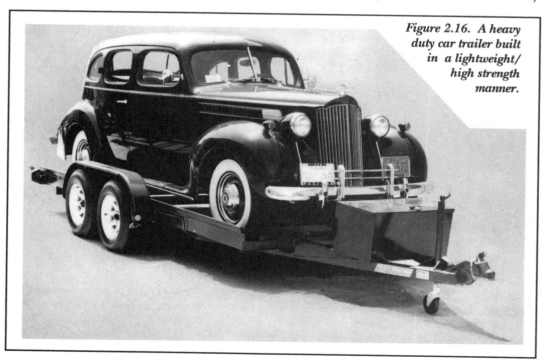

Figure 2.16. A heavy duty car trailer built in a lightweight/ high strength manner.

Figure 2.17. A mobile home frame without its home. Notice the twist at the forward end from just sitting.

are designed to depend largely on the addition of a house frame to provide stiffness and strength, particularly for twisting. The trailer of Figure 2.17 has no house to stiffen it. Thus the longer a frame like this becomes, the more twist and floppiness can be expected. Mobile home trailers are notorious for being designed to just do the job intended. It is fortunate they spend little time on the road and this is the excuse for their marginal nature. Used beyond the task of toting a home from mobile home park to mobile home park they often reach their limits quickly.

Careful analysis of weight requirements and materials before you begin construction will avoid these mistakes and give that needed opportunity to develop the best design. Strength with lightness must be the goal. For a given gross weight, the lighter the trailer, the more remains available for cargo. Although this seems obvious when mentioned, many people prefer to ignore it and their trailers become very heavy. Large semi-trucks are constructed mostly of aluminum—siding, framework, wheels—to save weight. A few parts, such as axles and main rails, are steel primarily because of cost and other trade-offs which make steel more desirable.

Steel shapes can, in fact, be formed to produce a lot of strength with lightness at a lower cost than aluminum and can often then compete with aluminum for lightness. *Volume 2* discusses this subject in more detail and the charts in its Appendix list properties for many shapes of material. Some of the formed steel shapes were developed, proven and used for many years by IRD Trailers.

By modifying the shape of the material rather than selecting formed hot rolled shapes, lighter sections are achievable. The more work one piece can do, the lighter your trailer will be. For instance, a car trailer often uses runners to guide the wheels. The runners can be placed on top of a frame resulting in additive runner and frame weights. Or the runner can be designed as a major structural member eliminating additional frame pieces.

Two purposes are served and considerable weight is saved. Material selection charts can be studied to develop a sense of important relationships and the manner in which the numbers change as the shape changes.

C. TRAILER TONGUE

Within the framework, certain areas require and deserve more attention than others. The design of the tongue is one of those areas. The tongue is not simply a way to attach the trailer frame to the tow-car; or, as is commonly thought, something used for pulling the main body of the trailer forward. Ah yes, it is indeed that, but it is much more. Other substantially higher loads exist that must be considered. Bending from downward weight, twist from bumps and side to side differential loading are a few worth mentioning. Ignoring these other loads, some of which are illustrated in Figure 2.18, can cause you to create a tongue incapable of supporting them. Be aware that an increase in tongue weight (often from load repositioning) or a rearward movement of the axle can substantially increase stresses on the tongue. Inadequate tongue design invites deformation and cracking as well as the potential for breaking. No question about it, this portion of your design deserves your undivided attention.

Attachment methods (tongue to the trailer body) are as varied as trailers themselves—on top of the frame, under the frame, butt welded to the front of the frame, or a continuation of the main frame rails (as in a boat trailer). The boat trailer's method of a continuous structure avoids a connection altogether since it is already one long piece. Assuming the material is large enough to handle the maximum loading and adequate lateral bracing is provided, it is, from my observation, an excellent solution. Using the same material the full length of the trailer adds a certain amount of additional weight in areas where less load is carried. However, welded joints and connections which may be more susceptible to fatigue and cracking are not lurking about. Unfortunately, in most trailer designs a continuous framework is not appropriate and a connection must be devised.

Tongue attachment points—to frame, to coupler—are considered "joints" in engineering terminology. Joints of any kind rank as the most difficult of design challenges. In addition to the ever present risk of separation, the potential for stress concentrations from holes, welds and changes in cross section, is much higher than with continuous material. Joints include connections made with welds, bolts or rivets and are covered in depth in **Volume 2**. In whatever way one configures a joint, the area should be carefully studied for not only the type of loads to be carried but the magnitude and direction of these loads along with the potential fatigue characteristics. Once the loading in the area is understood, a suitable

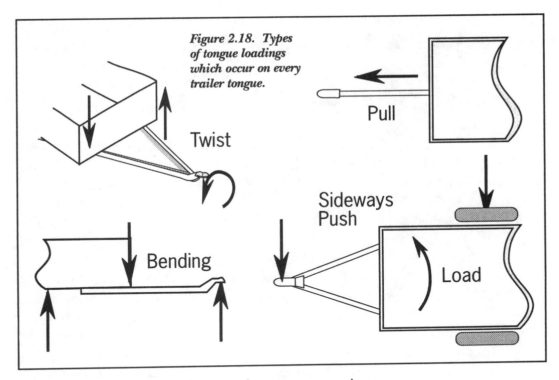

Figure 2.18. Types of tongue loadings which occur on every trailer tongue.

Twist

Pull

Sideways Push

Bending

Load

design and resistance to it is much easier to produce.

Tongues that are butt welded to the front cross-brace of the framework are quite common and often downright scary. In checking out trailers at the races, I frequently find cracked welds in this area. Recently, though, an even more alarming home-built trailer crossed my path at a traffic light. As it bounded through the intersection a 3 to 4-inch bending of the frame at the tongue-to-frame attachment was visible. I stared in amazement and decided to follow. When I pulled up next to this newly licensed trailer, I could see why its body gyrated like a hula dancer. Figure 2.19 is a side view drawing (I was caught without my camera) of the tongue connection as I saw it. Even though the tongue was triangular, from a top

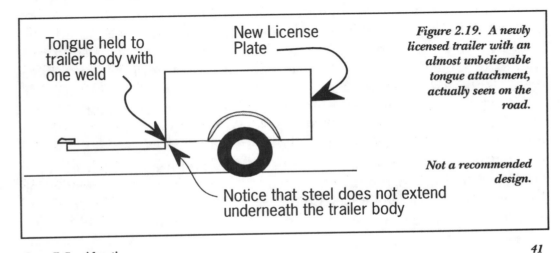

Tongue held to trailer body with one weld

New License Plate

Notice that steel does not extend underneath the trailer body

Figure 2.19. A newly licensed trailer with an almost unbelievable tongue attachment, actually seen on the road.

Not a recommended design.

Figure 2.20. A triangular tongue bolted to a T-Tongue member with only ONE bolt! The bolt is in the shadow A little bit of thought could certainly bring a more adequate solution to such an important connection.

Not a recommended design.

view, it attached to the frame at only a single point in the side view (a line in any other view). It was only a matter of time before fatigue of the tiny amount of weld area produced a most unpleasant surprise. I flagged the non-English speaking gardeners over to the side of the road and demonstrated their problem by pushing down ever so little on the front cross panel. The tongue-to-frame connection point dipped about 3-inches. Hopefully I communicated the solution and the trailer got fixed. Unfortunately this occurance is not all that uncommon since there are no standards or guidelines for anyone to follow; and licensing procedures have nothing to do with trailer design or adequacy.

Figure 2.20 is, in my view, another marginal tongue connection. The triangular legs are held to the straight leg with only ONE bolt—this is all that holds the coupler to the body of the trailer with its cargo. The U-bolts are used to resist bending and would do little to hold the center tube if that one center bolt broke. In addition the wiring access hole is placed in a highly stressed area just in front of the single bolt connection. Notice also there is no rubber grommet in the hole to insulate the wires from the sharp metal edges; not even a second jacket around the two wires for protection. A torched hole with its melted edges would be better protection for the wire. And a wire hole behind the bolt would create less weakening in an area most important for structural adequacy.

The tongue in Figure 2.21 is a T-tongue with a design which has totally ignored the loadings just described. Two spindly attachment points lacking any form of lateral support are all that hold this tongue to its body. The welds completely encircle the tubing eliminating any continuous

Figure 2.21. An underbody T-Tongue with two attachment points. Notice the lack of lateral bracing.

Not a recommended design or method.

material from front to rear. This weld embrittled circle make this area a high risk candidate for fatigue failure. In addition, the two drop down arms will need constant scrutinizing to detect the need for ever recurring repair.

Another tongue configuration to avoid is the one in Figure 2.22. Although triangular, it is so short one's tow vehicle could barely, if at all, make even the smallest of turns without a crushing event at the corners. The back of the coupler is only an inch or two in front of the spare tire's forward edge. This tongue's short length of about 2-ft is a serious potential problem for towability. Almost any speed above 35-mph could easily toss this little gem into uncontrollable sway. Let's just hope the tow vehicle is

Figure 2.22. A trailer with an incredibly short tongue. Loaded with only a minimal weight, improperly distributed, this trailer could easily rate in the number one danger category.

Not a recommended design.

LARGE. I have found truck bed trailers to require special considerations including sufficiently long triangular tongues. And to help balance the extra long rear overhang and forced higher CG, the longer the tongue, the better. The effect of these configurations is discussed in more detail in *Volume 2*.

Trailer tongues although very different from each other, generally conform to two standard formats—T-tongue style or triangular, sometimes called an A-frame tongue. The T-tongue can be a straight piece of tubing, pipe, or channel protruding from under the frame. This style of tongue usually attaches to a perpendicular cross piece. Twist, bending and shear loads must be carried with only one beam instead of two. To be as strong as a triangular tongue, a T-tongue must be a much stouter piece of material and be attached extremely well. In most instances it will also require diagonal reinforcing which sort of turns it into a triangular shape anyway.

In spite of the inferiority, T-tongues turn up on many trailers—light ones to mid-weights . . . and even on some heavy weights, as we have seen. Most trailer designs appear to have been built with the mistaken notion (already discussed) that the load is only pulled—not twisted, not bent, not vibrated. A T-tongue beam can resist these loads if it is big enough and the frame attachment is designed carefully. If the trailer is then never used beyond the tongue's capability, few problems are apt to appear. Unfortunately the risk of overloading a T-tongue is great.

On the other hand, a properly designed triangular tongue, for only a little more work and expense, will carry more of the prevalent loads in a more efficient manner than the T-tongue. Your trailer will be happier and so will you. Benefits of the triangular style tongue are numerous. The "load path" is smooth and far superior to that of the T-tongue. The loads at the coupler are pulling in an almost straight line from the spring-to-frame pick

Figure 2.23. Carrying a box can be likened to a trailer tongue design and give you a feel for the problem and its solution. Compare the difference in carrying a box held at the outside corners, which is well supported versus one carried at the center only.

up points. (See *Trailers—How to Buy and Evaluate*.) In contrast, the "sharp 90° turns" of the T-tongue design serve only to aggravate an already inherently weaker structure. Tongue leg material at the extreme outer points support just about any twisting of the trailer body. The one spindly leg of the T-tongue has little to resist this twist; thus loads on the welds (and structure) are very high. To illustrate this point, imagine carrying a box of steel parts about 30" long, as in Figure 2.23. Moving this box is considerably easier by lifting it with two hands, one at each end, rather than trying to balance it with one arm right in the center. Try it!

The trailers in Figure 2.24 and 2.25 are, in my view, closer to having tongues of secure and appropriate design. They are all triangular and all have couplers welded solidly onto their fronts. Couplers welded with both longitudinal, vertical and horizontal welds, as is possible with this design, are quite superior to couplers placed on top of the tongue legs using only longitudinal welds to secure them. The tongue closest to the viewer in Figure 2.24 is made of an angle cross section. This choice reduces the trailer's overall strength and is not consistent with the weight and mass and loading capability of the trailer body. The tongue's inadequacy may result in early wear and fatigue. Close examination of the tongue-to-frame point already reveals a small amount of distortion. This a relatively new trailer with fresh paint and comparatively little wear and tear. An additional piece of angle welded to the bottom of the existing angle to form a channel or boxed section would improve the strength of this tongue immensely.

Figure 2.24. Three trailer tongues with adequate and better than most, coupler-to-frame attachments. The front most tongue is made of angle, the second is channel and the third is tubing.

Figure 2.25.
Another government
trailer of massive proportions,
this time with a good long tongue.

The tongue of Figure 2.25 is well built and massive and fits the pattern of many found on government trailers. This tongue is made of two pieces of channel per side overlapped top and bottom and welded together into a tube shape. A tube of this cross section is strong in areas where the most strength is needed. The loads at the front spring perch are directed straight to the coupler via the triangular tongue legs. This is as it should be. The massiveness of this trailer is not particularly appropriate for consumer or even commercial use due to its deleterious effect on handling. Nor is the CG height conducive to high speed towing. But government trailers seldom exceed 45 mph and the ratio of tongue length to rear overhang helps to balance this trailer's other drawbacks.

The trailer of Figure 2.26 is another massive number. This shorty probably weighs more than it will safely carry. It is obviously a pick up bed complete with original axle, suspension, wheels and tires. The entire truck frame (the primary culprit of its overweightness) was left intact and cut far enough forward under the cab that bending it easily created the tongue—clever, huh? The coupler is solidly attached with all around welds and with a tongue a foot or two longer, it wouldn't be too bad of a design . . . except for its mass to cargo ratio.

The trailer of Figure 2.27 is another truck bed trailer with a similar massive tongue and frame. The variety of trailer frames constructable with a truck bed body bogles the mind. It is unfortunate that the majority of tongues are built so short that no compensation for the high CG and long rear overhang is incorporated.

*Figure 2.26.
A truck bed
trailer cleverly
constructed of
only the
truck's
remaining
frame.
Unfortunately,
the tongue is
rather short.*

*Not a
recommended
design.*

Triangular tongues, although superior to T-tongues, are not all the same, as you have no doubt just noted from the given examples. The nose angle of the triangular tongue can make a world of difference. Commonly the angle is 50°. This angle is popular because of precedence set by coupler manufacturers who make couplers with this angle. Asking questions around the industry, reveals that no one seems to have thought about any other angle. Why? I don't know. After studying the causes for trailer sway, I find the 50° angle unfortunate. It seems to encourage shorter trailer

*Figure 2.27.
Another truck
bed trailer with
a massive
under-structure.
The tongue on
this one is
longer than
most. With the
tire mounted on
the front body
panel, a
favorable
weight balance
is more easily
maintainable.*

*Not a
recommended
design.*

tongues and the use of straight axles, both of which have a less than desirable effect on stability. Economics and an industry steeped in tradition have made it difficult to influence changes.

Fifty degree couplers create a tongue that can be welded under the trailer bed, producing the most convenient coupler height for hitch attachment when a *straight axle* is used. Straight axles are popular because of reduced labor to manufacture and resultant lower cost. After all there are no bends or complicated welds, only machining of the spindles. This combination is the least expensive approach to trailer building, thus its popularity. The resulting tongue length of 3-feet (plus a little) is just the right length to miss the tow vehicle rear fender in a tight turn. In addition, a shorter tongue length facilitates storage in small places, hence the justification for this angle and the shorter tongue.

It seems to me the criteria for tongue length should emphasize performance at towing speeds rather than parking convenience. Figure 2.29 compares the difference in length of tongue for two different angles using the same rear width as the control dimension. Notice that the 40° angle permits a much longer tongue.

Low bed heights are also desirable for improvement in handling and the attendant ease of loading. With a drop axle and an under-the-frame tongue, the need to step the coupler up to a standard height of 17-in to 21-in becomes apparent. Methods employed to achieve this are numerous as can be learned by studying Figures 2.31 to 2.34. These entertaining examples are attempts to fill this need. Perpetrated no doubt by the lack of products to serve their function, these homebuilt solutions are also

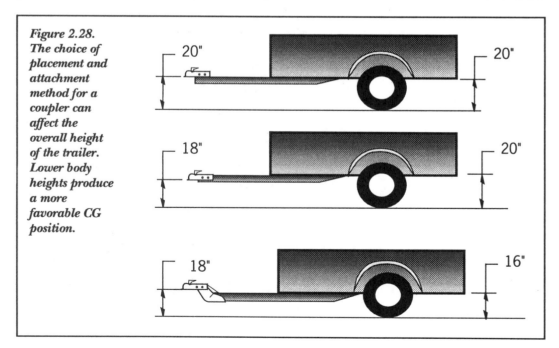

Figure 2.28. *The choice of placement and attachment method for a coupler can affect the overall height of the trailer. Lower body heights produce a more favorable CG position.*

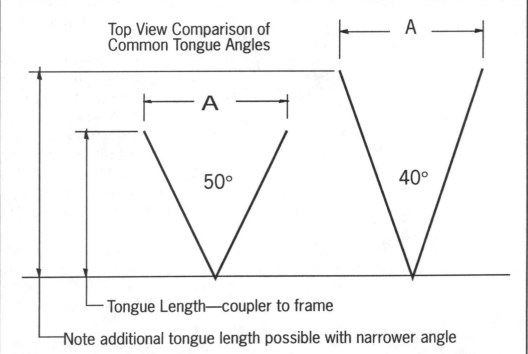

Top View Comparison of
Common Tongue Angles

A

A

50°

40°

Tongue Length—coupler to frame

Note additional tongue length possible with narrower angle

Figure 2.29. Comparison of two triangular tongue angles is shown here. The common 50° angle encourages a shorter tongue length, while the 40° angle simplifies the use of a longer tongue.

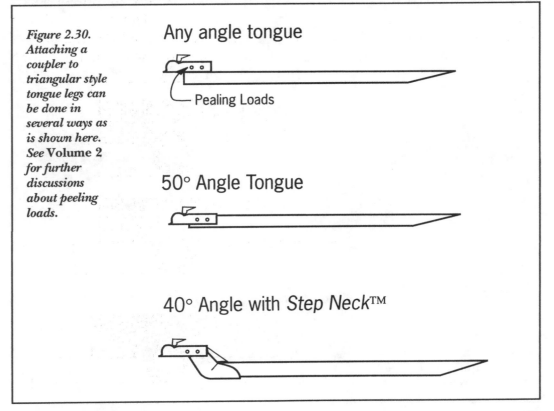

*Figure 2.30. Attaching a coupler to triangular style tongue legs can be done in several ways as is shown here. See **Volume 2** for further discussions about peeling loads.*

Any angle tongue

Pealing Loads

50° Angle Tongue

40° Angle with *Step Neck*™

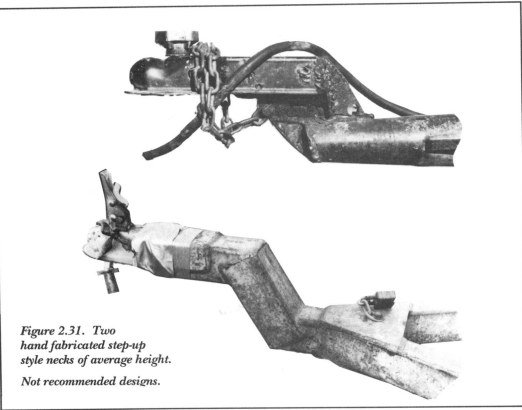

Figure 2.31. Two hand fabricated step-up style necks of average height.

Not recommended designs.

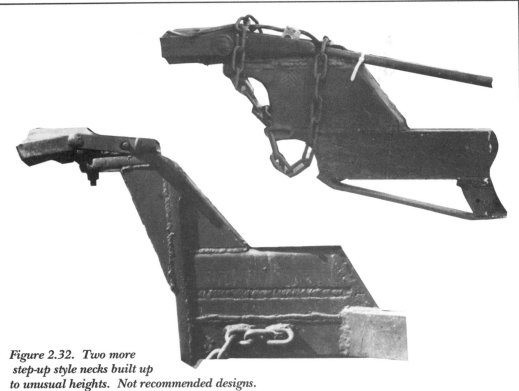

Figure 2.32. Two more step-up style necks built up to unusual heights. Not recommended designs.

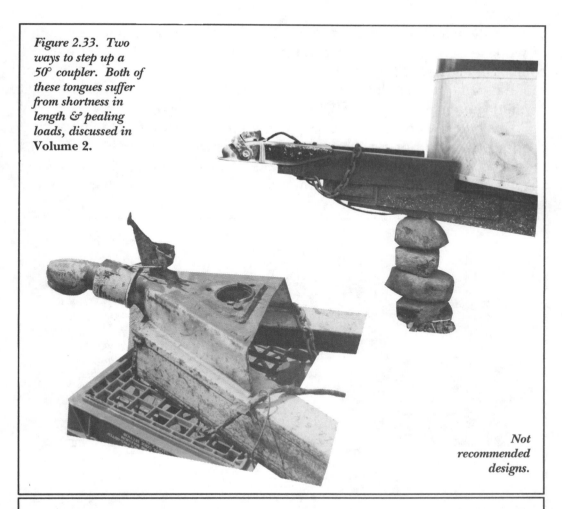

Figure 2.33. Two ways to step up a 50° coupler. Both of these tongues suffer from shortness in length & pealing loads, discussed in Volume 2.

Not recommended designs.

Figure 2.34. Besides extra height, extra length has been gained from this ungainly approach.

Not a recommended design.

structurally alarming. Each of these creations have required a large amount of work to achieve the stepped up height and lower bed. Even the 50° coupler of Figure 2.33, normally set up for wrap around welds, falls short of sound design practice since its fabricated block sits atop the two tongue legs permitting only the longitudinal welds for connection.

While few companies will take the time or risk of developing such a product, this author has thought about this problem extensively and produced a solution that not only provides a smaller angle encouraging the sought after longer tongue, but permits the dropping of tongue legs to create

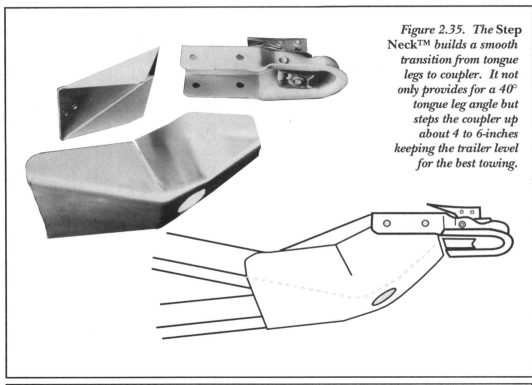

Figure 2.35. The **Step Neck™** *builds a smooth transition from tongue legs to coupler. It not only provides for a 40° tongue leg angle but steps the coupler up about 4 to 6-inches keeping the trailer level for the best towing.*

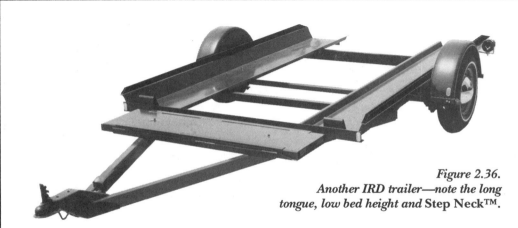

Figure 2.36.
Another IRD trailer—note the long tongue, low bed height and **Step Neck™.**

a lower center of gravity. This product, dubbed the *Step Neck™* is patented and shown in Figure 2.35. Compare its 40° angle to the common 50° angle tongue. The *Step Neck™* mounting also encourages use of a drop axle. Thus even though the bed is low, tongue legs are even lower and can extend under the main frame permitting a larger area for welding and fastening. Loads then carried by the weld (or fasteners) are also spread over a larger area and the load per inch of weld or fastener is then reduced, creating a stronger connection. The trailer in Figure 2.36 is an IRD creation using the *Step Neck™*. Note the long tongue and depth of drop down between the axles. If you are interested in further information about this product, contact the publisher for current status and availability.

D. AXLE PLACEMENT

To some this is the most important question of all. And certainly if not the most important, it is one of the most common questions. "Where to place the axle?" You may have heard friends talk about building trailers and their biggest conclusion is . . . "as long as the axle's in the right place, anybody can build a trailer." Yes indeed, axle placement is important . . . and the more poorly designed the trailer, the more important the axle placement. But it is far from the most important thing that determines

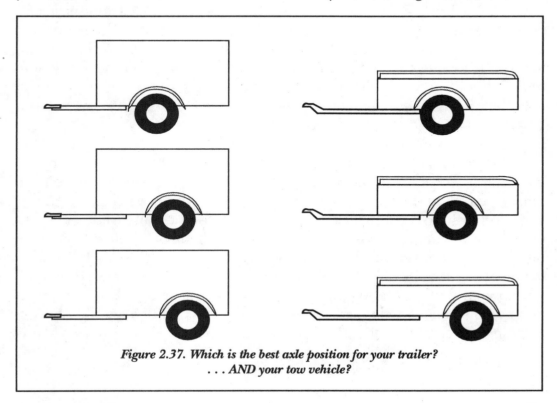

Figure 2.37. Which is the best axle position for your trailer?
. . . AND your tow vehicle?

success of a trailer. Too many things have to be co-ordinated for the trailer to be successful. Yet, you can't know how many people have called me on the phone and demanded I tell them simply and plainly where to place the axle on their recently built-at-home trailer. Maybe it was this question with the most complex and elusive of answers that inspired me to write this book.

Axle placement is very integrally a part of many other variables. It is a mistake to assume there is some simple rule to follow and some magic placement that will solve all problems. In the realm of physical possibilities, the axle can be placed just about anywhere along the bed of the trailer. The forward position is usually limited by the tongue or cross-brace at the back of the tongue. The rear hanger position is limited by the end of the trailer. With the newer style crank arm suspensions, an even greater latitude is possible.

We all have probably noticed or can easily imagine, that the axle's final placement determines tongue weight. Move the axle back and tongue weight increases. Move it forward and tongue weight decreases. If the axle is positioned exactly in the middle under the CG, it can be positioned such that no tongue weight at all is present. Please do NOT do this, as a friend did. Positioning the axle so the trailer is "perfectly balanced" with no tongue weight usually means you'll find the trailer tows "all over the road." This indeed is not the answer!

Some people, even some trailer manufacturers, have the mistaken notion that a trailer with a light tongue weight tows better, especially for smaller cars. A light tongue weight may be easier on the tow vehicle but to lighten the tongue on certain trailers could be disastrous. I do believe that a trailer should be designed so it can function well with a lightER tongue load, but this is very different than saying "light tongue weights tow better". *TRAILERS—How to Buy and Evaluate* discusses the many considerations necessary when planning axle placement.

Light tongue weights are certainly easier to lift and move around your yard. Just have a buddy jump on the back of your trailer to reduce tongue weight and try it. WAIT! Actually, it's better if he step up slowly and cautiously so the tongue doesn't fly upward or the trailer slide out from under him or you. Be sure he has something to hang onto so he won't slip off, either. Better yet, block the wheels, have everyone stand back and add inanimate weights SLOWLY to the rear until the tongue is lifted. Then find out how easy it is to move the trailer around. This experiment should be done with someone who has experience with this kind of activity. As with anything, I recommend the utmost of caution when attempting to move any trailer.

With tandem trailers, tongue weights can be made light enough so

Figure 2.38. An unusual but practical configuration for trailers with heavy tongue weights.

that the coupler sits entirely off the ground. This is convenient because a tongue jack and caster wheel is then not needed to move the trailer around. Building a trailer with this configuration invites trouble, though, because loading becomes critical. The missing tongue weight must be added with load positioning. An unloaded tandem such as this is possibly light enough to be towed by most cars without mishap, however, failure to compensate for this trailer's lack of tongue weight with loading could easily produce an unstable condition and unpleasant experience.

For small cars, light tongue weights can be very important. But if the weight is too light, the resulting instability of the trailer can have a devastating effect. A light tongue weight in and of itself is more apt to produce instability than a heavy tongue weight. But it is all very, very relative and a trailer can be cleverly designed to tow well with a lighter tongue weight.

The real question is, "How light?" My experience with IRD Trailers is that many of them would tow well with as little tongue weight as 3% of the gross, well below the government tested and recommended minimum of 8%. The IRD trailers though had many features that contributed to towability. The majority of trailers built today do not duplicate the IRD blueprint and often attempt to lighten tongue weight by moving the axle forward and leaving all other parts the same. This is NOT the answer!! Bear in mind that no matter what the tongue weight there is always some critical speed where instability occurs. The real trick is to move that critical speed to a point well above towing speeds. Please understand what you're doing before you move the axle forward.

In many cases heavier tongue weights do improve towability . . . of the trailer. However, the tow vehicle definitely has to be sufficient to handle it, not only from the stability standpoint but from its other towing capabilities including braking, gearing, drive train and engine power. An interesting solution to the tongue weight question is shown in Figure 2.38. The tow vehicle for this trailer is virtually relieved of the tongue weight as that weight is placed on the 5th wheel style dolly. Almost half the weight of the trailer and its cargo is held by the dolly while the other half is held by the other set of wheels which have been positioned entirely to the rear. And so you rightfully ask, "If this is such a good approach, why are more of these trailers not made?" One reason is the general misunderstanding of benefits to be derived. I can only speculate that another is consumer resistance to additional expense, since more hardware and labor is required to build such a trailer. Laws also prevent individuals towing such a device without a special class license. This also appears to be a relatively costly design project, which may deter new ventures into uncharted territories.

In general, though, and for any given trailer, there is a resulting tongue weight for each trailer/tow vehicle combination which is optimum. Too much tongue weight tends to make the tow vehicle unstable, but too little makes the trailer unstable. The result is the same in either case—an unstable, possibly uncontrollable system. *Volume 3* presents a system of analysis which looks at these extremes and *TRAILERS—How to Buy & Evaluate* summarizes these factors in easily understandable form. Axle position, along with the resulting weight distribution, is one of the factors included here. The axle position and resulting tongue weight is part of the challenge of designing your own trailer. Finding the precise combination for a trailer AND its tow vehicle is only one step in the entire process.

CHAPTER 3.

SUSPENSION SYSTEMS

A. Axles

B. Spindles

C. Hubs

D. Suspension Types

    Leaf Springs

    Attachment Hardware

    Torsion & Crank Arm Styles

E. Wheels & Tires

F. Trailer Brakes

    Electric

    Hydraulic

    Mechanical

Suspension components along with basic ones fit together with all the frame pieces to create the whole—a trailer with character and integrity. Suspension includes hubs, axle, brakes, springs, wheels and tires. Other components include coupler, fenders, lights and a myriad of accessories. Certain components have a major part in determining capacity, while others are mere add-ons. As your design progresses, you will be answering every question imaginable about each and every component. The more you know about each of these parts, the more certain you will be about combining them into a safe, satisfying and useful product.

Start by selecting the right parts to build your trailer—not just any old axle, hubs, springs and coupler—you know, the one Uncle Harry had stashed behind the shed. Selecting the most appropriate components will produce the most desirable results. Remember you're building something that will travel down the freeway at 55-65 mph. Please, for all our sakes, take the time to know what you're building.

Secondly know the technicalities of each component. The more you know about products available on the market, their limitations and their correct use, the easier it will be for you to make the most appropriate selection for the job. Knowing capacities and dimensions of a part is important. Understand also that a newly selected or revised component may modify dimensions or choices you have previously made. Rework your design until all the elements are coordinated. As you study the next few chapters the mystery of many components will gradually evaporate.

Still, your end result may not be perfectly coordinated as to capacity. One part will always be weaker or stronger in relation to some other part. Listing the different components and their separate capacities will provide some insight regarding this puzzle. At first, the trailer's true capacity appears difficult to assess. Finding the weakest link can be confusing since different components support different things. The true capacity may well be the weakest link. But just what is the weakest link?

Let's see how this works. Figure 3.1 lists several components on a typical trailer. The maximum gross weight of this hypothetical trailer is 6720 pounds, the maximum net load is 4720 pounds. What is the difference? And why is the gross not 7000 pounds as the hubs and axle would indicate? The **net load** is what you carry on top of the trailer, the **gross** includes the trailer weight as well as the cargo. Let's look at this more closely. The axle carries the framework, the springs and the load on top. The springs carry just the frame and load. While the hub carries the axle, springs and frame and rests on the tire. The weight of the trailer—suspension and framework—must be deducted from the gross to know the capacity remaining for cargo. As you can see from the figure, each component in the chain carries something different and can be rated

Figure 3.1. *Capacities & weights of components on a typical trailer.*

Description	Capacity per Unit	Quantity of Item	Total Capacity
Maximum Gross Load			6720-lbs*
Maximum Net Load			4720-lbs
Axle Capacity	3500-lbs ea	2ea	7000-lbs
Spring Capacity	3750-lbs/pr	4ea	7500-lbs
per inch of deflection			
Hub Capacity	3500-lbs/pr	2pr	7000-lbs
Wheel Capacity	1700-lbs ea	4ea	6800-lbs
Tire Capacity	1680-lbs ea	4ea	6720-lbs*
Coupler Capacity	6000-lbs ea	1ea	6000-lbs
Frame Capacity	5500-lbs	1ea	5500-lbs
			(over & above frame weight)
Trailer Frame Weight	1500-lbs		
Suspension Weight	500-lbs	(wheels•tires•axles•hubs•springs•hardware)	
Gross Trailer Weight	2000-lbs	(before load is added)	

Recommended tongue weight: 8% to 15% or 540-lbs to 1050-lbs

NOTE: If expected tongue weight is less than 9%, other aspects of the trailer must be designed very carefully!!

accordingly. Examining each component in this manner provides a fairly accurate physical limitation of your trailer and its parts.

As with many things, though, there are a few traps. All too common is the mistake of rating the trailer at whatever the axle will carry: 7000-lbs in this case. Too many people (some manufacturers included) know the axle/hub rating—and that's all they know. They then assume this is the rating of the trailer. For example, with 2 axles rated at 3500-lbs, they state the trailer will carry 7000-lbs. Only after being challenged will they concede that the 2000-lb framework and suspension will bring the actual carrying capacity to 5000-lbs. In fact, in many cases, the tires do not have sufficient rating for even the 7000-lb gross. And the down rating is even greater, as in this case to 6720-lbs (4720-lbs net).

Another trap is finding selection of a few items easy and then resting on your laurels and assume everything else is easy. Lack of attention to the more difficult areas can easily produce an unroadworthy trailer. The component selection process involves a complete understanding of the whole system, many reworks of the overall design, and a thorough integration of all the parts into the whole.

A. AXLES

The *axle* is an important and integral part of the suspension. It is the main horizontal cross-wise bar that carries the vertical downward loads from the frame and cargo. Tension through it also serves to keep the spindles in a horizontal position. The *spindles* are placed at each end of the axle. *Bearings* slide onto the spindles and carry the hubs. Onto the *hubs* are bolted the *wheels* (or rims) with mounted tires. The *tires* rest on the ground, supporting the entire load from the trailer weight and cargo. Figure 3.2 illustrates terminology and the direction of forces on each suspension part as the loads transfer from one component to the next. Each part is an important element as it transfers loading through the system.

Axles come in all shapes—round, square, rectangular, tubular, solid bar, drop, straight—from dimensions of 1-1/4-in up to 5-in square. The most common cross sections used on axle material are illustrated in Figure 3.5. Axles come in many lengths and capacities, too. Figures 3.3 and 3.4 show some of the more common axle styles available. Popular spindles are shown in Figure 3.10.

Terminology used with *straight* and *drop axles* is shown in Figures 3.3 and 3.4. The *overall* length is taken from the two outer-most extreme points on the axle. This often translates to the overall width of the trailer you are building. And many wheel widths are set up to end close to this plane. The *axle track* falls between the inner and outer bearings and is used by travel trailer manufacturers that have varying wheel off sets or can accept a different axle. By retaining a standard track, they are sure the tires will fit under the fenders of their coach body. *Between-the-drops* dimension is useful for defining the outside frame width. By subtracting 1/2-in per side (1-in overall) from this dimension, a maximum frame width providing minimum overhang can be achieved. *Spring centers* are the points where the spring centering holes are drilled. These are predrilled only with a solid bar axle. If the axle is tubular, drilling weakens the axle far too much. Thus you will receive a small bracket to weld on yourself for aligning these holes. Depending on the axle, the brackets take on several different designs. Two styles of these weld on brackets can be seen in Figure 3.9. The *axle drop* is used to define the dimension from the hub center to the spring. To know this accurately, it is necessary to query your supplier as to how they determine it. Most manufacturers correctly use a dimension from *center* of hub to *center* of axle bar. With this dimension given, one must know the axle OD (outside diameter) to determine the additional height to the top of the spring. If your supplier uses an axle drop from *center* of hub to *bottom* of axle, it may mislead you into thinking the two drops are the same, when, in fact, you have *less* drop with this axle.

There is one advantage to this method. You don't have to do an additional calculation to add in the extra height. Just be sure to get a definition.

The axle carries as much as, or more than, any single frame member; this assignment and duty makes its strength especially important. The axle's strength and capacity are dependent on many factors: tube or bar size, spring mounting position, spindle designation, and method of fabrication. Most axle manufacturers state the axle rating somewhere in their sales literature. The more reputable companies even attach a capacity plate to the axle. When you use the axle within the range stated and as recommended you can count on the strength and expect the axle to last a long, long time. Selecting an axle knowing it will be overloaded is a mistake and an outright invitation for trouble—so don't do it. Overloading can shorten useful life significantly and create the environment for a break at some unexpected future date.

Axle strength can be determined in a number of ways: 1) by bending test, 2) by fatigue test and 3) by calculations. The most practical method is by calculations—since the axle is spared and the amount of work is considerably less. However, if you plan to manufacture axles in any quantity, testing is also important and should be considered seriously.

The type of calculations necessary are described in **Volume 2**. As a preview we have performed some simplified calculations here. As you will find, the first step is to calculate the applied load—this includes both trailer and cargo. Once found, it should be split in half and applied to the spring mounting positions at one end of the axle. Figure 3.6 shows the resulting load, shear and moment diagrams for a load of 2000-lbs with an offset (spring perch to tire) of 10 inches. Once the bending moment and material

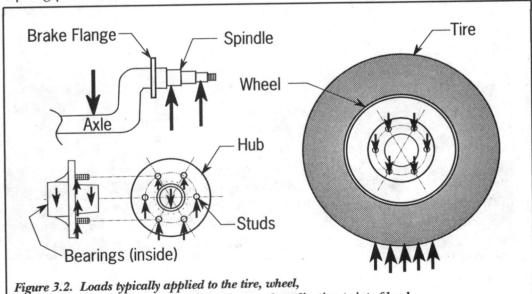

Figure 3.2. Loads typically applied to the tire, wheel, hub and spindle. Arrows indicate directions and application point of load.

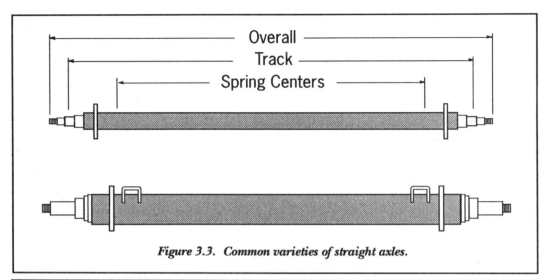

Figure 3.3. Common varieties of straight axles.

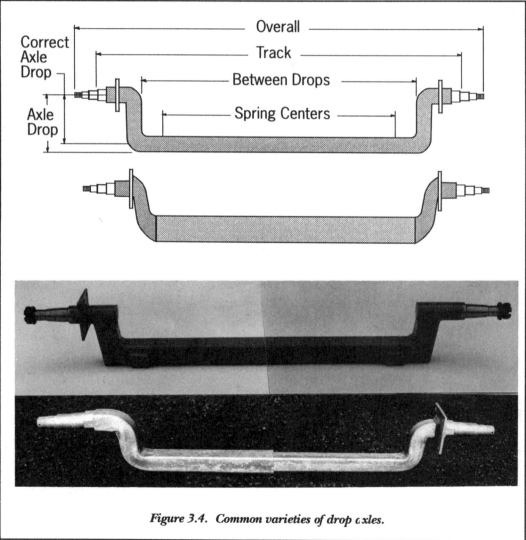

Figure 3.4. Common varieties of drop axles.

of choice (steel, aluminum) is known, the required moment of inertia for the load can be calculated. Knowing this, an appropriate material cross section can be selected. Figure 3.7 shows the calculations to select such an axle for this 2000-lb load. Although choices of material other than solid bar are available, we have used only 1-1/2-in solid bar as an example.

If you already know the axle size and want to determine its strength or carrying ability, a slightly different approach to the problem is required. Figure 3.8 determines the carrying ability of a 1-3/4-in axle with a 10-inch overhang and then compares a 9-in overhang with an 8-in overhang. "Plow steel," which has a tensile stress of 110,000 psi and a yield point of 60,000 psi, is assumed as the material. As explained in **Volume 2**, the yield stress is reduced to an allowable of (.6) x 60,000 = 36,000 psi. Stresses below this allowable point are regarded as being within the elastic range. (NOTE: It is not proper to use the ultimate strength—we want to know when it will bend, not break.) The final allowable load with an overhang of 10-inches is then 1786-lbs/side, or 3572-lbs total. With an overhang of 8-in, the allowable load increases to 1984-lbs/side or 3968-lbs total—an 11% increase in strength! The moral of this story is to shorten your axle overhang

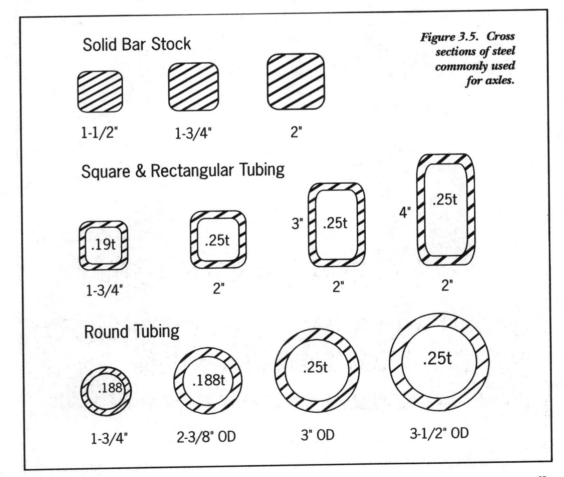

Figure 3.5. Cross sections of steel commonly used for axles.

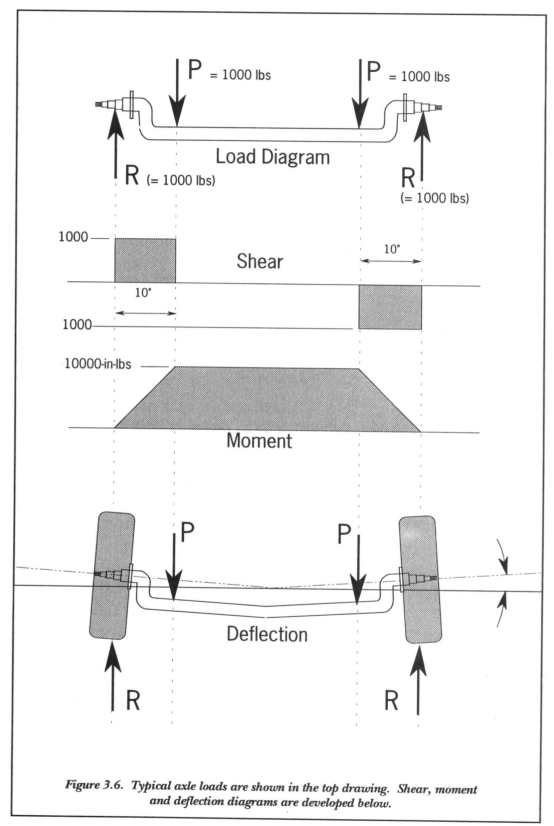

Figure 3.6. Typical axle loads are shown in the top drawing. Shear, moment and deflection diagrams are developed below.

Figure 3.7. To find the required material size for an axle to carry a 2000 lb load, the steps shown below are necessary.

From the moment diagram of Figure 3.6, we know that M = 10,000 lbs.
Given the material as "plow steel," we can then use an allowable elastic stress of
s = (.6) 60,000 psi = 36,000 psi.

To find the size material for an axle that will support
2000 lbs with an overhang of 10-in, we proceed as follows

$$s = \frac{Mc}{I} \text{ rearranges to } \frac{I}{c} = \frac{M}{s} = Z$$

$$Z = \frac{M}{s} = \frac{10000 \text{ in-lbs}}{36000 \text{ lb/in}^2} = \frac{I}{c} = .278 \text{ in}^3$$

The basic flexure formula (see *Volume II* for more discussion of this formula)
is shown in the box above. Thus we have

$$Z = .278 \text{ in}^3$$

The material chosen must have a larger section modulus than our calculated Z of .278 in³.

Looking through the tables in Appendix A of *Volume II*,
we find a material size with the following numbers:

For a 1.5-in solid square bar,
Z = .563 in³
I = .4219 in⁴
c = .75 in

For this material, note that the value for Z exceeds the minimum allowable by
.563 in³/.278 = 2.025 times.

Since the bending moment is less for an axle with a shorter overhang, the axle carries less load and the configuration is stronger as can be seen by the chart below:

Axle size & Z	Overhang (in)	Moment (in-lbs)	Req'd Z (in³)	Design Factor
1.50 (.563)	10	10000	.278	2.025
1.50 (.563)	9	9000	.250	2.252
1.50 (.563)	8	8000	.222	2.536
1.50 (.563)	7	7000	.194	2.902

If instead our 2000-lb load was placed at a 7-in overhang, our required Z becomes .194. We then have a design factor of 2.902. This calculation should help you understand why we recommend a frame as wide as possible thereby positioning the axle overhang as short as possible.

***Figure 3.8.** Knowing that we have an axle of 1-3/4-in square, the question is often asked, "How much will it carry?" To answer this the steps below can be used.*

We start with a solid bar of "plow steel," 1.75-in square where,
$$I = .7819 \ in^4$$
$$Z = .893 \ in^3$$
$$s = 0.6 \bullet (60,000) = 36,000 \ psi$$

Using the reduced allowable stress (as discussed in *Volume II*), we first find the maximum bending moment, M, this size material will carry.
Using the basic flexure formula again, we solve for M as follows:

$$s = \frac{Mc}{I} \text{ rearranges to } M = \frac{I}{c} s = Z \bullet s$$

$$M = (.893 \ in^3) \bullet (36,000 \ lb/in^3)$$

$$M = 32,148 \ in\text{-}lbs$$

Adding a dynamic load factor of 1.8 gives us an answer consistent with industry capacities. This is applied on top of the already reduced stress level of 36,000psi. Therefore, we must immediately reduce this moment to an allowable range, as follows:

$$M = \frac{32,148 \ in\text{-}lbs}{1.8} = 17,860 \ in\text{-}lbs$$

With a 10 inch overhang, this moment is equivalent to a single force or load determined as follows:
(where F = Force, d = Distance, M = Moment)

$$M = F \ x \ d \ \text{ and, } F = \frac{M}{d} = \frac{17860 \ in\text{-}lbs}{10 \ in} = 1786 \ lbs/side$$

Total Load on the axle = 2 x (1786) = 3572-lbs

To determine the allowable load with a different overhang, we change the value of d, and calculate the allowable load for each length. The allowable moment for each calculation remains the same since the material does not change. The results are shown below:

Axle size & Z	Overhang (in)	Moment (in-lbs)	Allowable Load (lbs)
1.75 (.893)	10	17860	3572
1.75 (.893)	9	17860	3968
1.75 (.893)	8	17860	4465
1.75 (.893)	7	17860	5103

These calculations determine the point at which the axle can be expected to reach 60% of yield stress with a 1.8 dynamic load multiplier. This is an interesting calculation because 1.75-in axles are rated at 3500-lbs. With a 10-in overhang, the axle capacity appears to just meet the standard rating. With a shorter overhang, the allowable load actually increases. However, I still recommend using as short an overhang as possible (7-in) and using the 3500-lb rating. Age, rough roads and slight overloads are a continual threat. Short overhangs don't cost anything but are a considerable gain.

by positioning the frame side rails out as far as possible.

Strength can be estimated with calculations—by far the easiest method of arriving at a decision and getting you into the ballpark. Calculations, however, do not replace the testing process, they only preceed it. With welded connections and complicated load paths (commonly found on tubing axles), testing is especially important.

A bending test will give the static strength of the axle. Merely place the axle in an H-Frame press and note the force at which permanent deformation occurs; i.e., the metal bends and does not return to its original position. To obtain an accurate reading, the set-up should be configured so that the push points are at the hub center and the spring mounting holes (Figure 3.3), just as it would be on a trailer. Loading it otherwise gives erroneous results. All in all this is an easy test. Unfortunately, it will destroy the axle you're testing. In addition, the data obtained is useful only if your trailer will sit still during its loaded life.

A fatigue test is more difficult but will more accurately reflect an axle's use and ultimate capacity. This test also has a good chance of destroying the axle. A load that will fatigue an axle to breaking is usually much smaller than the static load to bend it. Stress concentrations which result from holes, bends, welds or changes in shape reduce load carrying ability. The exact amount of load reduction is difficult to predict and may even vary from axle to axle. Hence, the axle you choose for this test should be relatively free of those things—but it should be representative of the axle group you are checking out.

The effect of stress concentrations from shape and the axle's expected load carrying ability can be determined by testing several axles in this way. A test fixture similar to the one used in the bend test is necessary. Designing such a test fixture can be quite a project in itself and is often wisely left to an independent testing lab as is the actual testing. Instead of the static load from the H-Frame press, the load must be set up so it can be applied and released, applied and released, applied and released for at least 1 million cycles . . . or until the axle breaks at some smaller number of cycles. After destroying a few samples in this fashion, the load at which that style of axle will last forever is eventually defined. Because this procedure more closely imitates the axle's environment, a much more accurate figure of an axle's strength is attainable.

Beyond the calculation and testing process, there are certain configurations of an axle that will basically improve strength and resistance to fatigue; and others that won't. Stress concentrations worsen resistance, while a smooth, straight, uninterrupted section improves it. Figure 3.9 illustrates configurations which *worsen* fatigue resistance:

Figure 3.9. Axles can be built in many ways. Some methods are stronger than others as shown below.

Configurations that weaken an axle.

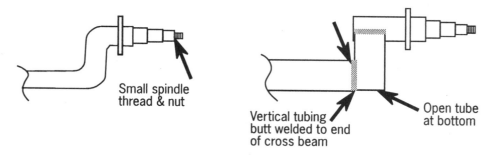

Small spindle
thread & nut

Vertical tubing
butt welded to end
of cross beam

Open tube
at bottom

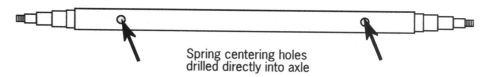

Spring centering holes
drilled directly into axle

Configurations that strengthen an axle.

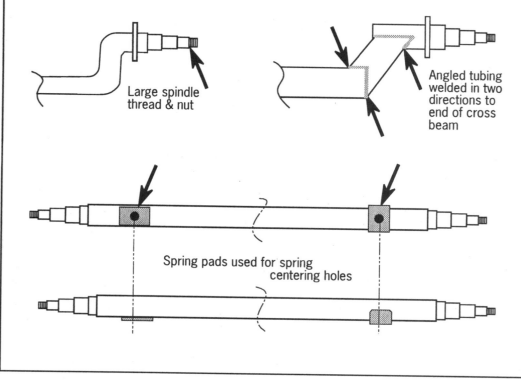

Large spindle
thread & nut

Angled tubing
welded in two
directions to
end of cross
beam

Spring pads used for spring
centering holes

1) End nut threads are much smaller than the outer bearing diameter—usually requiring a 3/4-inch nut rather than a 1-inch nut;
2) Welded connections are used to weld a spindle to a tube to make an axle without consideration for the load paths;
3) Spring centering holes are drilled directly into the material;

Strength, reliability and fatigue resistance of an axle will *improve* if:

1) An end nut close to the same diameter as the outer bearing—usually a 1-inch diameter;
2) A solid bar bent axle is chosen rather than one of poorly designed welded construction;
3) A spring centering hole is welded onto the axle with a plate (called a spring pad) rather than drilled into the axle;
4) Welded axles are heat treated to normalize the uncontrolled hardening and built-in stresses from weld heat.

If this discussion sounds like welded axles are to be avoided, you may be right. Welded axles certainly have more areas where failure can begin and should at least be checked out carefully. On the other hand, welded axles do afford one advantage. They do not require special equipment or tooling, and are therefore very cheap to manufacture and can be built by just about anybody. Solid bar axles, which have been used for many years, do not have the features which invite the stress concentrations of welded axles. As discussed in **Volume 2**, welding's inherent risk of lack of penetration, undercuts which create invisible stress concentrations and the change of material properties right next to the weld, can be lethal in a component as important as an axle. Consumers should be especially wary of welded axles and should be warned to carefully scrutinize the axle on the trailer they are considering purchasing.

Don't get me wrong, most manufacturers whose primary business involves axles and whose designs and procedures are obviously well thought out are not part of this category. Welded axles if carefully designed and tested can be effective and endure as required and expected. Capacities need to be checked carefully and construction supervised with an eagle-eye. To gain the advantage of flexibility and the low cost of a welded axle while maintaining a decent amount of structural integrity, forged drop spindles have recently found their way to market. These axles although welded, are fabricated under very controlled conditions and appear to be rated conservatively. This axle style is shown in Figure 3.4.

BT Spindle • 1800 lb Capacity

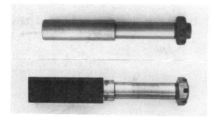
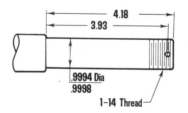

84 Spindle • 3500 lb Capacity

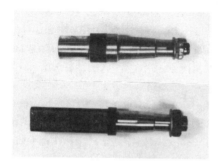
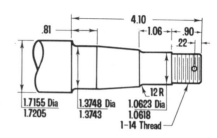

42 Spindle • 5200 lb Capacity

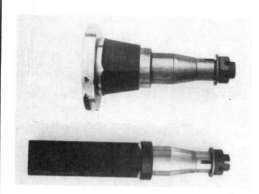
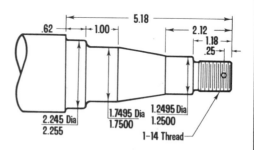

Figure 3.10.   Three of the most common spindles used in the trailer industry.   Capacities range from 1800-lbs to 5200-lbs per pair.   The center spindle is often called the Universal spindle.

Considering their importance and the gravity of the single duty assigned to them, axles must be attributed a high priority when it comes to defining adequate strength.

B. SPINDLES

A *spindle* is a part of the axle. It is a machined part whose primary purpose is to support the bearing races (see Figure 3.11) for the hub. Figure 3.10 shows the most common spindles used in the trailer industry for capacities of 1800-lbs, 3500-lbs and 5200-lbs. While other spindles are available for various reasons, higher capacities and special uses, the capacities shown here cover just about any application, up to extra heavy duty trailers. You would be doing yourself a favor by selecting one of the more common grinds shown here, since replacement bearings, seals and hubs are very easily found and readily available from bearing stores and many trailer supply outlets.

Spindles for trailers are quite different than automobile spindles. The more reliable ones are much "beefier" than auto spindles. Considering the difference in load requirements, this should be expected. An automobile spindle carries 1/4 of a 4000-lb load (plus or minus) or about 1000-lbs. A typical midrange trailer carries 1/2 of 2000 to 3500-lbs (1000 to 1750-lbs). This loading difference is also important when selecting wheels and tires.

Spindles are rated for a specific load using similar techniques as used for computing axle strengths. Spindle strength is usually figured and rated separately from the axle. In addition to just plain overloading, spindles can be weakened by excessive heat (from lack of bearing grease or rust), and/or use of positive offset wheels which can increase the bending moment at the spindle. This offset also increases the *overhang distance*—not something we want to do, as you may have guessed from a few pages back. With a little attention, these situations can be avoided and spindle life increased. Designing a new spindle is not something everyone should undertake considering the bargains in the ones currently available. Besides being inexpensive for what is provided, optimum spindle design is best left to automotive engineers and bearing experts who have had many years of experience in this field.

Spindles are machined to a precise diameter such that the bearing ID will slide on easily with the right amount of clearance. If you experience difficulty installing a bearing, it may be due to a burr on the spindle, which can be removed with a very light touch from a file or piece of sandpaper. Be sure to then clean the surface with a solvent soaked rag before attempting to slide the bearing on again (small filings can accelerate bearing wear).

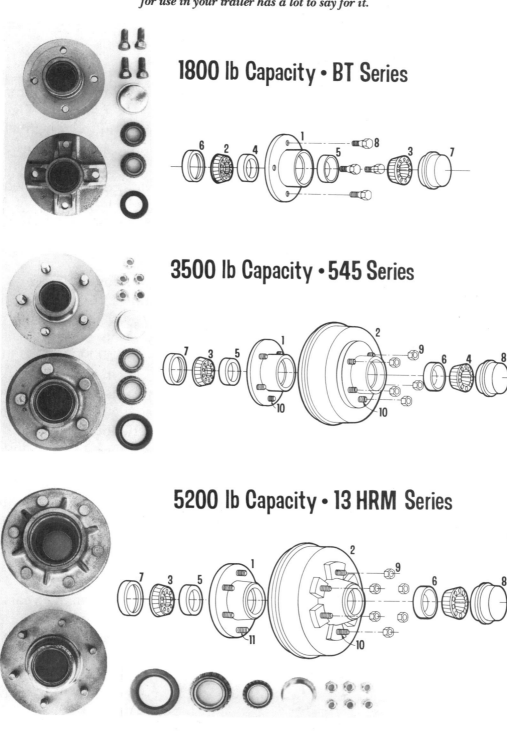

Figure 3.11a. *The most common hub & drum assemblies available, shown with bearings. Because of their popularity, selecting one of these hubs for use in your trailer has a lot to say for it.*

1800 lb Capacity • BT Series

3500 lb Capacity • 545 Series

5200 lb Capacity • 13 HRM Series

C. HUBS

The **hub** provides the mounting surface for the wheel. The hub spins on the **bearings** which slip over the **spindle**. The bearings, although separate parts, are usually associated with the hub. When brakes are used, the brake drum is attached to or is integrally a part of the hub and spins with it. Figure 3.11a shows the elements common to hubs as they slide onto a spindle. Coordinating the capacities and dimensions of all these elements is an arduous task, but must be done to ensure a reliable system. The load capacity of the assembly is dependent on many factors: bearing size, bearing position, cross sectional area of the hub and of the spindle, and design of the hub flange. Fortunately, the capacities of hubs, brakes and bearings are usually determined by the manufacturer and all you need to do is specify your desired capacity and abide by it.

The automotive and trailer industries use tapered roller bearings in hubs almost exclusively. Prior to tapered rollers, ball bearings were quite common. For a given size, tapered roller bearings have much greater load capacity and have become the preferred choice for wheel bearings. A process of elimination has resulted in a relatively standardized set of hubs and brakes as shown in Figure 3.11. Common ratings for hubs are 1800-lbs, 3500-lbs and 5200-lbs/pair as shown here.

A bearing is never designed to last forever, even under ideal conditions. **Bearing Life,** or **Rating Life,** is subject to many criteria but is basically the specific time that 90% of a group of identical bearings will last before a fatigue spall or pit damages the surfaces of either the cup or the cone. Life, load and speed are interrelated; for instance, doubling the load,

---

Figure 3.11b. These numbers refer to the bearings and hubs in 3.11a.

BEARING PART NUMBERS

Spindle Style Options	Bolt Circle	Inner Bearing Race (Cup)	Roller (Cone)	Outer Bearing Race (Cup)	Roller (Cone)	Grease Seal National Number	Dust Cap Diam
BT-12	4 on 4"	L44610	L44643	L44610	L44643	34823	
	4 on 4-1/2"	L44610	L44643	L44610	L44643	34823	1.9"
	5 on 4-1/2"	L44610	L44643	L44610	L44643	34823	
84	5 on 4-1/2"	L68111	L68149	L44610	L44649	58846	
	5 on 5"	L68111	L68149	L44610	L44649	58846	1.9"
	6 on 5-1/2"	L68111	L68149	L44610	L44649	58846	
42	6 on 5-1/2"	25520	25580	L67010	LM67048	35544	
	8 on 6-1/2"	25520	25580	14274A	14125A	35544	2.44"

reduces life expectancy to approximately one-tenth. Doubling the speed cuts the life in half. In addition, the amount of lubrication and temperature are a part of the **Life Adjustment Factor**. Here less lubrication and higher temperatures tend to reduce a bearing's life.[12]

Thus bearing capacity and life are a function of applied load as well as the bearing's environment. In normal use, depending on tightness of the nut, trailer bearings heat up just from rotation. This heat can soften the grease which, depending on temperature and type, can then leak from a worn or weak seal gradually reducing the amount of grease in the cavity. After a trip hot hubs cool, at which time condensation can occur.[15] Trailers left sitting exposed to the elements are also vulnerable to moisture, as are boat trailers backed into the water for launching their cargoes. Any moisture in the hub creates rust—small particles which can then disrupt the required roller action of the bearing. Rust filled grease creates more friction and the potential for more heat. Hot bearings with little or no grease get even hotter . . . and so the cycle continues.[15] Proper re-greasing at appropriate intervals is one of the best solutions for longer bearing life and retained load carrying ability—two thousand mile intervals is a common suggestion in trailer owner's manuals. After this discussion, you can see why it's not such a bad idea.

Bearing cavities should be kept full of grease. To assist with this and keep the elements out, **bearing protectors**, which replace the dust cap, are available. *Dutton Lainson's* version provides a zerk fitting for quick and easy re-filling of the hubs, a 4-psi pressure relief valve and a higher quality rear grease seal. *Bearing Buddy®* uses a 3-psi pressure inside the hub as

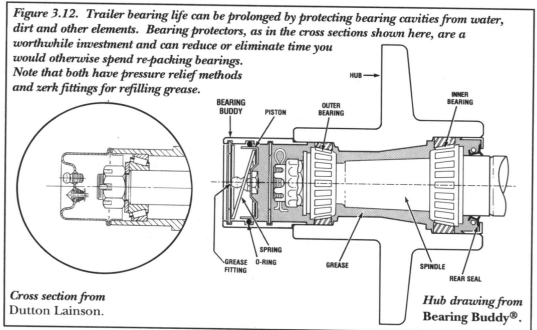

Figure 3.12. Trailer bearing life can be prolonged by protecting bearing cavities from water, dirt and other elements. Bearing protectors, as in the cross sections shown here, are a worthwhile investment and can reduce or eliminate time you would otherwise spend re-packing bearings. Note that both have pressure relief methods and zerk fittings for refilling grease.

Cross section from
Dutton Lainson.

Hub drawing from
Bearing Buddy®.

well as the refiller zerk fitting and claims the standard seal is adequate; however, a very high quality seal is available as an accessory. The *Sure-Lube* system provides for complete refill of the cavity without removing the bearings, since the pressure relief valve is at the end of the special drilled spindles. Properly filled and maintained bearing protectors reduce or eliminate the need to re-pack bearings. Be sure to check the instructions included with each product. Figure 3.12 shows cross sections of two kinds of bearing protectors in place.

It is important to note that specs for some hubs state a maximum wheel size. For instance, some BT hubs (see Figure 3.11) are rated for a maximum 12-in wheel. Others will take a maximum 13-in wheel. To place a 13-in wheel on a 12-in rated hub is mere folly and a request for future problems. For example, a BT hub rated at 1800-lbs but with a maximum 12-in wheel requirement effectively reduces capacity to that of a 12-in wheel, where ratings commonly range from 800 to 1100-lbs—not the 1800-lbs of the hub. The flange design is often the deciding factor as to this type of capacity. Notice the gusseting on the back side of the BT and the 13 HRM hub flanges in Figure 3.11. This style hub results in a much stronger unit for the amount of material used.

D. SUSPENSION TYPES

"Springs? Who needs springs? I had a trailer for 10 years. It towed great. Low to the ground. Easy to load. It never had springs!" *TRAILERS—How to Buy & Evaluate* shows several examples of such trailers. "Of course we had to constantly re-weld the coupler, axle and all corners of the frame". If you don't mind this extra expense, bother and potential risk of inopportune failure, then no, you don't need springs to make a trailer operate. The wheels still roll, it still hooks to the tow-car and your cargo can still be loaded. And there are plenty of trailers around without springs to support your conviction. But springs do make life easier for everybody—cargo, fellow drivers . . . and in the long run, even you.

The primary purpose of springs is to cushion the load fed into the frame of the trailer and subsequently the merchandise on top. If your cargo has little or no value, such as garbage, a trailer without suspension will certainly get you to the dump and probably back. On the other hand, if your cargo or trailer has value, you may want to reconsider and decide that springs are an important and necessary part of the trailer. Trailers with springs spend much less time in weld repair shops having fatigue cracks repaired than those without springs. If you already own a trailer without springs, an investment in a welder will quickly pay for itself. So will an investment in springs.

Tandem trailers, though, pose a special problem when built without springs. One axle or the other ends up being overloaded. This happens when a ball height too low pulls the nose of the trailer downward, thereby lifting the rear axle off the ground as in Figure 3.13. On the other hand, a hitch ball height too high, lifts the front axle off the ground. Even with a hitch ball height coordinated with the trailer coupling height, this see-saw continues on dips and rises in the road playing havoc with axle ratings, especially if axles are installed with the intent to carry only half the load. In reality, the axle sees one-half the load only part of the time and, unfortunately, ALL the load some of the time, as the weight shifts from front axle to back axle. The only solution to this see-saw is to install springs of some sort—and there are several from which to choose.

Suspension—Leaf Springs

Until recently, trailer suspension systems in the U.S. have been pretty much standardized since trailers were first towed behind automobiles. Leaf springs, the product of least resistance, are and have been cheap and readily available from many junk yards in all shapes and sizes. Although the use of junk yard springs are seldom appropriate for manufactured trailers, the pattern stuck. And in light of few other options, trailer manufacturers found themselves requesting automotive springs for their creations. Hence, the unanimous swing to this suspension. Figure 3.14

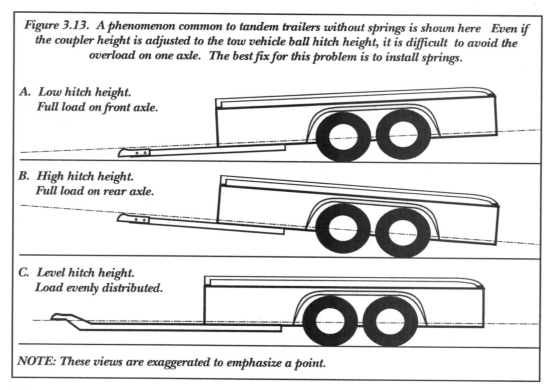

Figure 3.13. A phenomenon common to tandem trailers without springs is shown here Even if the coupler height is adjusted to the tow vehicle ball hitch height, it is difficult to avoid the overload on one axle. The best fix for this problem is to install springs.

A. *Low hitch height.*
   Full load on front axle.

B. *High hitch height.*
   Full load on rear axle.

C. *Level hitch height.*
   Load evenly distributed.

NOTE: These views are exaggerated to emphasize a point.

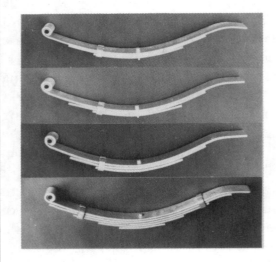

Figure 3.14. Leaf springs of the styles shown here have been in common usage for many years. Standardized dimensions have fortunately found their way to trailer springs (except for the junk yard variety). The number of leaves and the material thickness are used to vary the capacity as can be seen by studying the list of springs shown below. The lower part of the list is for standard style springs while the upper refers to slipper style springs. The springs are pictured with increasing numbers of leaves. To determine the actual capacity one needs to reference the part numbers as shown in the list below.

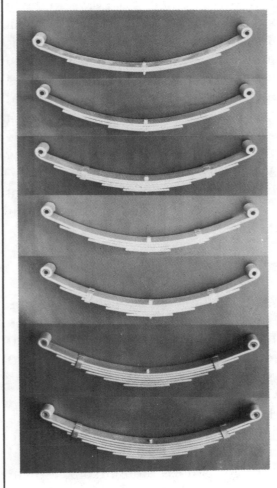

SPRING SIZES/CAPACITIES

Spring Part No	Capacity per Pair	Number of Leaves	Leaf Thickness
BT25-9	900	3	0.250
BT25-12	1200	4	0.250
BT25-15	1500	3	0.312
BT25-22	2250	3	0.360
BT25-25	2500	5	0.312
BT25-30	3000	4	0.360
AS-3	900	3	0.250
AS-4	1200	4	0.250
AWS-2	1500	2	0.360
AWS-3	2250	3	0.360
ATS-5	2500	5	0.312
AWS-4	3000	4	0.360
AWS-5	3750	5	0.360
AWS-6	4500	6	0.360
AWS-7	5200	7	0.360
MHS-8	6500	7	0.401
MR-3	6000	3	0.500

illustrates the two general styles typically installed on new trailers. The standard two-eye springs are the same style as automotive springs and have been around the longest. The slipper style is a fairly recent development for trailers. Slipper springs are more economical and in some ways provide a gentler load transfer from spring to frame.

Selecting the correct springs is much easier if you know something about shapes, capacities, dimensions, what's on the market and what works best where. A chart of typical spring capacities and their corresponding sizes is also shown in Figure 3.14. Except for very large capacities, the width for most trailer springs is 1-3/4-in. Standard two-eye springs have an eye to eye dimension of 26-in while the slipper is designed for an overall of about 25-in with the slipper length about 3-in to 4-in long, as the figure shows. Capacities of leaf springs are varied by changing the thickness of the material and the number of leaves, while retaining the same basic dimensions. These standardized dimensions certainly simplify installation.

Spring ratings are generally given in the number of pounds that will make two springs deflect 1-in, i.e. pounds per inch usually written as lbs/in. This is a good basic number to use. Bear in mind that this 1-in deflection is from a static load. As you might guess, a slight overload will merely compress the spring more, to 1-1/4-in or 1-1/2-in, even 2-in. This is not a problem until the trailer is towed down the road where the effective load can double (or more) when a bump is hit. And, yes, when this occurs, it means the load is instantaneously twice or thrice the static load and the springs are compressed accordingly. If the load is within the capacity range, the springs merely compress. When the springs have plenty of room for deflection, the frame and cargo are cushioned. If the load is beyond that capacity, bottoming of the springs is a very likely scenario and the result is as if the trailer were unsprung; thus, the frame and cargo take a beating.

Suspension—Attachment Hardware

Springs are useless without a way to attach them to the frame and the axle. The hardware shown in Figures 3.15 through 3.17 are typical of the variety of parts needed to accomplish this task. Figure 3.17 will help you identify and name each of the individual parts. Figure 3.18 through 3.20 illustrate the standard assembly order and dimensions for the three most common leaf spring configurations—single axle slipper, single axle two-eye, tandem axle two-eye springs. Notice that only a few parts are welded to the trailer frame while the rest are bolted in place. Springs themselves are always bolted, never welded. Springs are a highly heat treated special formula steel whose properties remain intact unless embrittled with heat from a weld. Welded spring steel will fatigue and crack from only a small number of load cycles—probably your first trip out. So please don't weld springs. (Sorry about the lecture, but I have seen springs welded.)

Of the welded parts—**hangers, spring eyes and slipper tubes**—specified dimensions can certainly simplify the installation process. Figure 3.18 through 3.20 give dimensions recommended for these installations. It is possible that your spring dimensions are slightly different than the ones shown here, so be sure to ask your supplier for installation instructions. Additional **fitting gussets** and **diamond doublers** to reinforce these parts are also an inexpensive way to gain extra strength. Calculations indicate the need for more weld on these parts and a knowledge of stress concentration and experience from farm equipment reinforce that assessment. Hanger manufacturers never seemed to want to make hangers with longer bases; hence these solutions were sought. Patterns for these simple, highly effective weld-on parts are soon to be available from *Techni-Visions*.

Bolted parts include **rockers, link plates and springs**. Grade 5 **serrated bolts**, 9/16-inch diameter by 3-inch length are used for this purpose. If these bolts are installed with the **lock nuts** to the outside, loosening is much more easily detectable during periodic inspection. Any necessary repairs or replacements can then be performed. If the lock nuts which are used on these 3-inch bolts are removed, their locking ability should be rechecked before being re-used. We found many that could not be used more than once. The expense to replace used nuts with new lock nuts is minimal and well worth the trouble to order a few extra pieces. If you cannot obtain more of these mechanical style lock nuts, *Loctite* can be used temporarily but the surfaces have to be extremely clean for this method to be effective. Given the environment and the non plated bolts, this cleanliness may be difficult to achieve. Thus, a new lock nut should be installed as soon as possible. With the nut to the outside, this replacement is relatively easy.

The axle is attached to the spring with **five hole plates** and **U-bolts** of a size to fit the axle width and shape. Five-hole plates come with various hole spacings to accommodate different axle sizes—1-1/2-in, 1-3/4-in, 2-in, 2-1/4-in, 2-1/2-in, 2-3/8-in round, 3-in round. U-bolts selected with these plates must be long enough to extend past the spring height and the axle height, yet short enough not to extend past the bottom of the wheel. U-bolts that extend past the wheel rim are illegal in most states, since a flat tire will permit them to gouge the pavement—a disagreeable occurrence. **Non-locking nuts** and **spring washers** are used on the bottom side to hold the spring, axle and five-hole plate together. These require a good amount of tightening—enough to flatten the lock washers. Hardware for springs and axle assembly can usually be ordered as a set, which greatly simplifies this myriad of dimensions and parts. Even simpler are the new torsion suspensions, our next topic.

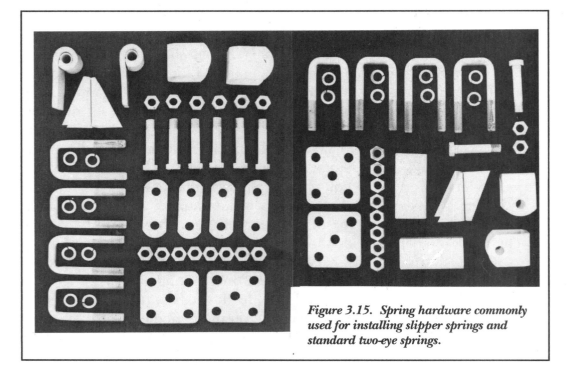

Figure 3.15. Spring hardware commonly used for installing slipper springs and standard two-eye springs.

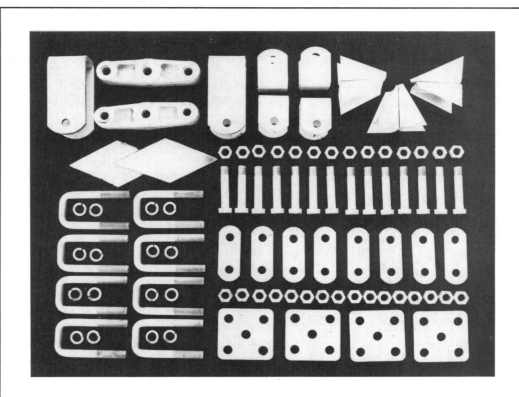

Figure 3.16. Hardware necessary for installation of tandem style suspension systems. A tri-axle includes additional hardware for the third spring and axle.

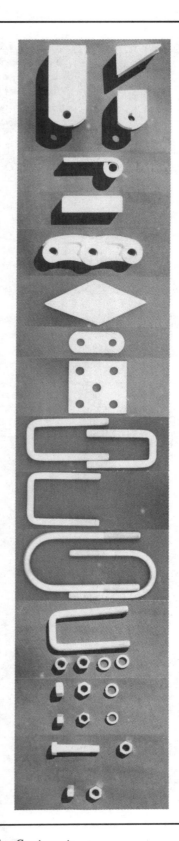

Figure 3.17. Spring hardware parts & pieces used for attaching leaf springs to the framework and to the axle are identified below.

    A. **Tall hanger, for tandem springs**
    B. **Fitting gusset**   C. **Short hanger**

    D. **Spring eye, for two-eye springs**

    E. **Slipper tube**

    F. **Tandem rocker**

    G. **Diamond doubler**

    H. **Link plate**

    I. **Five-hole plate**

    J. **U-bolts of various lengths and widths to accommodate many different axle shapes and sizes—**

        1-3/4square, 1-1/2"square,

        2-3/8" square,

        3" round, 2-3/8" round,

        2" square.

    K. **Hex nuts with lock washers, 9/16"**

    L. **3-inch serrated capscrew, 9/16"**

    M. **Lock nut, 9/16"**

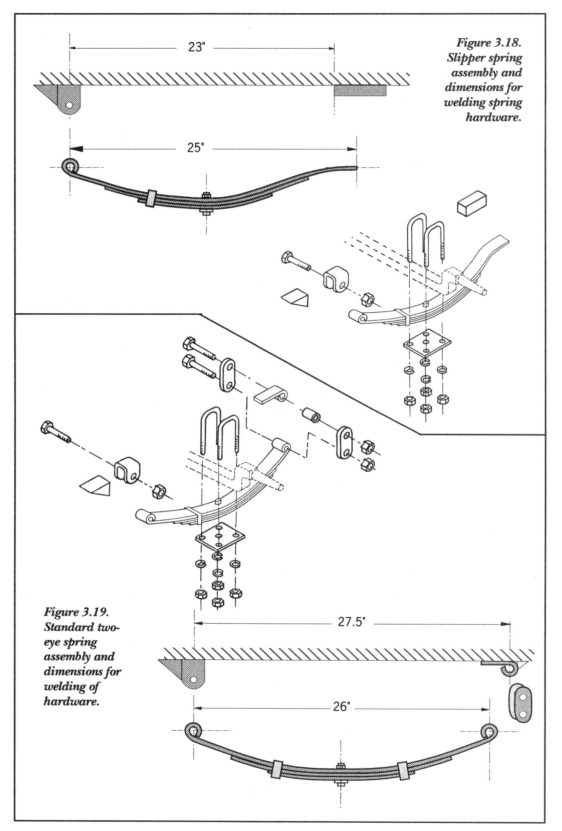

Figure 3.18.
Slipper spring
assembly and
dimensions for
welding spring
hardware.

23"

25"

Figure 3.19.
Standard two-
eye spring
assembly and
dimensions for
welding of
hardware.

27.5"

26"

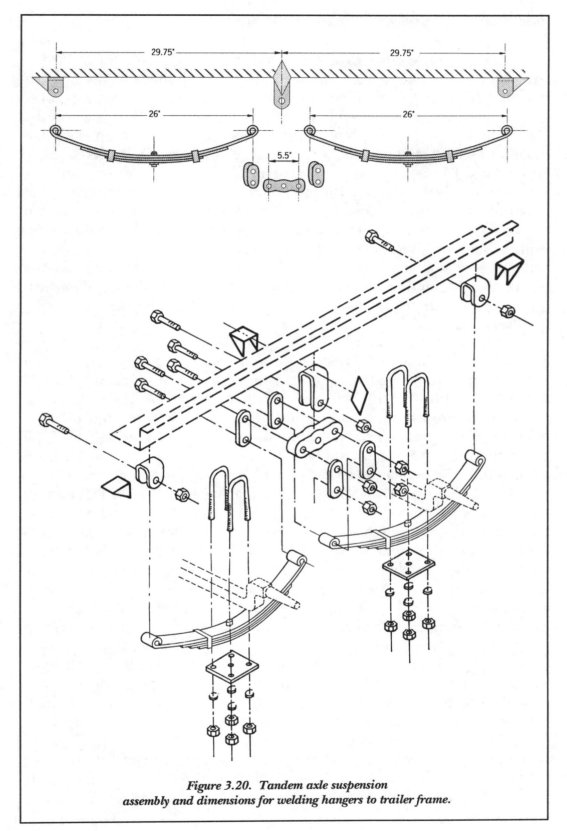

*Figure 3.20. Tandem axle suspension
assembly and dimensions for welding hangers to trailer frame.*

Suspension—Torsion & Crank Arm Styles

Torsion style suspension/axle options are available for the more adventuresome. Figures 3.21 through 3.27 illustrate these suspensions in more detail. Usually the spindle is welded to a crank arm that is pivoted about a cross-bar, which often but not always, extends the full width of the trailer. Springing is most often provided with rubber (or a compound) that squashes as the crank arm rotates. This style suspension has been used in England and European countries almost exclusively for many years and has just recently begun to filter into U.S. markets. The advantages over conventional suspensions are numerous. Torsion suspensions are independent, more compact and their proponents claim a smoother ride. With a full width cross-bar, the axle can also act as part of the frame, adding a structural component with less weight. The cross-bar then has two functions—axle and frame cross member—in contrast to a common leaf spring axle which crosses the full frame width but serves only to hold the spindles horizontal.

Most of the torsion suspensions available operate as shown in Figure 3.21 where the crank arm twists and the rubber spring compresses. Full independence from side to side is easy to achieve with separate housings. Since the springs are inside the axle, lower CG's are possible while retaining a good amount of ground clearance. The myriad of parts necessary to install a conventional suspension are overwhelming by comparison to the few nuts and bolts or welds required to install a torsion suspension. This equates to a simple, trim and neat suspension.

As with any product, though, there are limitations. Note that most of the suspensions shown in Figure 3.23 are made of rubber. A "rubber rod" is used on several, while two styles use molded rubber which is vulcanized to the twisting arm. While the compound of rubber for each may be different, rubber is unfortunately a substance that is known to deteriorate with time. Rubber can also take a set; i.e. only partially return to its original position when compressed with a load. Rubber can also be temperature sensitive. At elevated temperatures, softness can contribute to excessive wear; at extremely low temperatures, the amount of springing is apt to be reduced. Depending on your requirements, these factors may have little influence. Rubber is inexpensive and may well be just the answer especially with the variety of properties available with different compounds. This is a good place to check more carefully with your supplier.

The use of independent axle housings with these suspensions is in some ways a great advantage since it gives a lot more options for the frame. However, if either rubber or steel is installed without adequate cross support, the trailer frame can bend in the center creating more negative

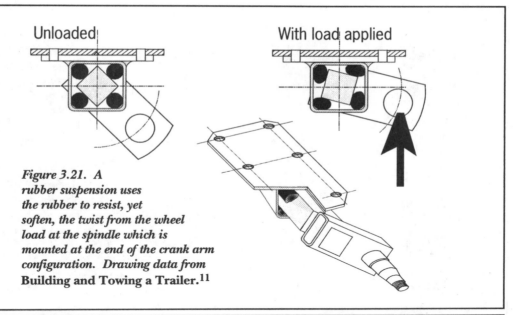

Figure 3.21. A rubber suspension uses the rubber to resist, yet soften, the twist from the wheel load at the spindle which is mounted at the end of the crank arm configuration. Drawing data from **Building and Towing a Trailer.**[11]

Unloaded

With load applied

Figure 3.22. A pair of rubber suspensions mounted on an unloaded trailer. Note the slight negative camber of the crank arm in comparison to the housing.

camber at the wheels. In addition, if the rubber suspension center twist bar is inadequately supported at either end, a slight amount of negative camber results, as shown in Figure 3.22. This lack of support can also contribute to an uncomfortable amount of body roll as a response to road conditions. Bumps deflect all suspensions, but a rubber suspension can also be deflected in an undesired direction.

Steel torsion suspensions are more expensive but can eliminate some of the disagreeableness of the rubber. Steel does not deteriorate with age or from chemicals (diesel fuel, animal wastes. . .). It also bends in a more predictable manner and only in the direction permitted. Cross sections for two known styles are shown in Figure 3.24. Currently only the *Torax* is on the market; however, by the time you read this book both may be and

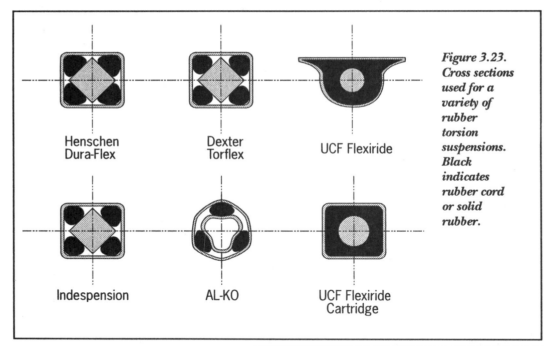

Figure 3.23.
Cross sections
used for a
variety of
rubber
torsion
suspensions.
Black
indicates
rubber cord
or solid
rubber.

Henschen
Dura-Flex

Dexter
Torflex

UCF Flexiride

Indespension

AL-KO

UCF Flexiride
Cartridge

searching out the whereabouts may be worthwhile time spent.

Overall handling with any torsion suspension is claimed to be smoother and better from that with the conventional leaf spring suspensions. A common claim is that these suspensions eliminate sway. This claim contradicts the recent dramatic increase in trailer accident rate in England coincident with an increase in the trailer speed limit of 10mph.

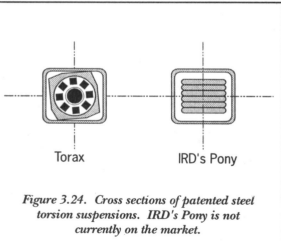

Torax

IRD's Pony

Figure 3.24. Cross sections of patented steel torsion suspensions. IRD's Pony is not currently on the market.

Most of the accidents have been attributed to trailer sway.[14] A brief look at **Volume 3** tells us the only suspension component in the sway equation is tire cornering stiffness. We can also note here that sway has a lot to do with mass and weight distribution as well as trailer configuration. But a suspension to substantially eliminate sway needs to be correctly chosen and installed on a properly designed and otherwise sway resistant trailer.

However, some of the claims made by torsion suspension proponents have been substantiated with the use of an independent testing lab. A smoother ride, as detected by the tow vehicle, results when the longitudinal and horizontal loads at the hitch are lower. The *Henschen* axle was tested to determine longitudinal and horizontal hitch loads in

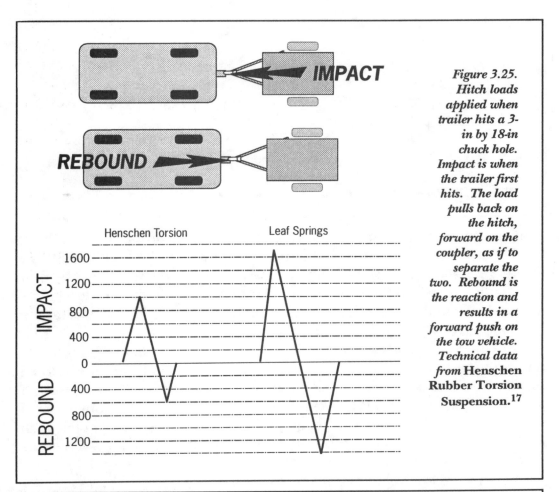

Figure 3.25. Hitch loads applied when trailer hits a 3-in by 18-in chuck hole. Impact is when the trailer first hits. The load pulls back on the hitch, forward on the coupler, as if to separate the two. Rebound is the reaction and results in a forward push on the tow vehicle. Technical data from **Henschen Rubber Torsion Suspension.**[17]

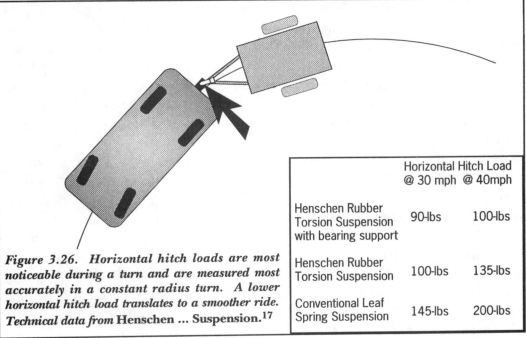

Figure 3.26. Horizontal hitch loads are most noticeable during a turn and are measured most accurately in a constant radius turn. A lower horizontal hitch load translates to a smoother ride. Technical data from **Henschen ... Suspension.**[17]

	Horizontal Hitch Load	
	@ 30 mph	@ 40mph
Henschen Rubber Torsion Suspension with bearing support	90-lbs	100-lbs
Henschen Rubber Torsion Suspension	100-lbs	135-lbs
Conventional Leaf Spring Suspension	145-lbs	200-lbs

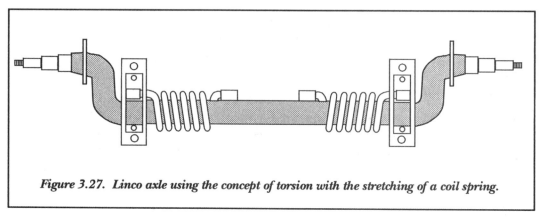

Figure 3.27. Linco axle using the concept of torsion with the stretching of a coil spring.

comparison to loads from a trailer using the standard leaf spring suspension. Loads transmitted through the hitch ball were measured and are shown in Figure 3.25 and 3.26. The longitudinal load test involved an 18-in by 3-in deep chuck hole and the subsequent recording of the initial impact and its rebound. Note that the *Henschen* axle produced much lower loads at the hitch for this test.

Horizontal loading becomes most apparent in cornering and is tested on a constant curve radius. The horizontal loading with a conventional suspension is almost twice as large as with the Henschen rubber torsion axle. As described in **TRAILERS—How to Buy & Evaluate**, conventional suspensions, because of their geometry, tend to increase horizontal hitch loads. The independence of torsion axles eliminates this added yaw force and again the loads are lower at the hitch. Thus a smoother ride as detected by the tow vehicle can be substantiated.

A slightly different torsion suspension which is not independent and which uses torsion in its springing mechanism is shown in Figure 3.27. This arrangement has no roll flexibility—both wheels must move up and down together relative to the trailer frame. Thus, the ride may be unduly harsh, as both sides of the trailer "jump" when only one wheel hits a bump. In addition, as the load is pulled down by gravity from weight or a bump, the coil spring wrapping the axle is pulled tighter and tighter. These coil springs will tighten only so far, at which point the trailer becomes springless. These axles are recommended for relatively static conditions, such as found with a piece of equipment—a generator, a welder, a steam cleaner. Where the potential for varying loads, especially an overload exists as with a general use flatbed or box trailer, these axles are not recommended. For loads that are relatively constant, though, these axles are clean and easy to install.

Torsion suspensions appear to be the way of the future. They are trim and neat with much less paraphernalia required under the trailer. Hangers, bolts, nuts, washers, links and rockers may well be a thing of the past. Lower trailer bed heights with increased ground clearance are easier to achieve. And installation is definitely simplified. If torsion suspension manufacturers are able to get together and settle on some standardizations to benefit their customers, they will make it easier to obtain replacements and design trailers. Users of conventional suspensions currently enjoy these advantages. Making the change to the torsion suspensions will be much easier if customers aren't locked into one supplier. Standardizations should include outside tubing dimensions, mounting methods, spindle sizes and spring rates. The Appendix lists addresses for several companies currently manufacturing and/or distributing torsion style suspensions. If you're designing a new trailer, these suspensions are well worth considering.

E. WHEELS & TIRES

Tires are of supreme importance. Selecting the correct ones for your application is a task well worth your utmost attention. Tires may appear simple; after all, there are four on your automobile and everybody uses them. But sorting out all the sizes, shapes, numbers, treads, services and compounds can be an arduous task for a trailer. The number of combinations is limitless . . . and confusing to boot. Then there's the wheel and all of the available bolt patterns, widths, offsets, disk styles and its capacities. It is easy to appreciate a manufacturer's dilemma in stocking specialized wheels and tires, especially if several models of trailers are part of their line. Not only are size and fit an issue, but tires can have a profound effect on the stability of your whole rig. More information regarding the effect on stability from the tires can be found in *TRAILERS—How to Buy & Evaluate*.

In general, tires used for trailers must have high cornering stiffness which usually translates to stiff sidewalls. Trailer service tires, designed for use on trailers only, can be counted on to contain the features necessary for towing. They have stiff sidewalls and a cross section similar to the old "78 series" tires. These are the best choice for your trailer. If standard passenger car tires are to be used, their capacity must be reduced 10% to obtain a realistic carrying capacity when used on a trailer.

Radial tires have elicited a lot of controversy. They have been used on trailers with some success, even though their sidewalls are considered to be not stiff. Government testing has shown radials to be superior in cornering stiffness, although it does seem to depend greatly on the individual brand of tire and the actual load. Radials also hold the road to a certain point, generally above the load for an equivalent bias belted tire. The disadvantage is that when the higher give out point is reached, road holding decreases as cornering rate increases whereas a bias belt tire will continue to hold at its generated higher rate.[18] Inflation pressure is also important—marginal or under-inflated tires have reduced cornering stiffness and definitely reduced load carrying ability. Be sure to check this out before towing. *Volume 3* discusses these load and tire characteristics in more detail.

Circumstances unrelated to your choice often dictate the tire you will use—such as a garage full of used tires, or "my friend has a good deal" or . . . whatever. Just be sure you are determining the capacity correctly and taking into account the trailer's eventual use and complete weight when you attempt to arrive at the actual capacity required. Tire capacities are marked on the outside face, making it easy to assess their capacities.

Insufficiently strong wheels can crack and come apart. Wheel failures are not something to risk. A standard passenger car rated at 4800-lbs gross will have 4 wheels with a capacity of 1360-lbs each. Two of these on a trailer give a toting capacity of 2700-lbs less 10%, or 2430-lbs—a rather marginal number for most trailers—and certainly not the tire to use with a 3500-lb axle. Wheels, (or rims), are very often the determinate of overall capacity. Wheel capacities are not as easy to assess as tires, but they are extremely important. It is folly to use a tire rated at 1680-lbs and a wheel at 1300-lbs. Wheel capacities are sometimes stamped on the inside rim and should be checked if you have any questions. The best source for this information is the manufacturer.

Black steel wheels are a popular choice and usually readily available; they can be fitted with hub caps for a little class. These wheels with no markings and a 5-hole pattern can range in capacity from 1100 to 1800-lbs. Unfortunately, the hub cap nodes on wheels vary considerably and finding hub caps to fit can sometimes be a real chase. Painted steel

Figure 3.28. White spoke wheels and black wheels with hub caps are great for trailers. Spoke wheels are available from Industrial Tire Co (see Appendix).

spoke wheels (shown in Figure 3.28) dress up the looks of your trailer quite a bit. They also are devoid of hub caps, eliminating the confusion in attempting to get the right size and fit. Commonly used on trailers these days; they not only look nice, but provide a place to wrap a locking chain. Fancy magnesium wheels also look great but are expensive and an invitation to thieves. The available wheels and tires are constantly changing and being upgraded. Whatever you buy, it is important to understand and know the rated capacity.

F. TRAILER BRAKES

Brakes are an integral part of the suspension system and are used to slow the wheel with friction. When brakes are applied, the shoes are pushed outward against the drum where the friction between the expanded shoes and drum slows the wheel. The backing plates, shown in Figure 3.30, which carry the brake shoes are bolted to a flange, Figure 3.29, which is welded to the axle. The drum, shown in Figure 3.31, is usually cast as an integral part of the hub and provides the surface for the shoes to rub against.

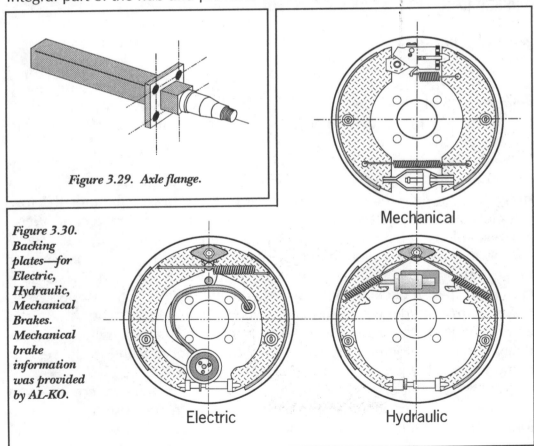

Figure 3.29. Axle flange.

Mechanical

Figure 3.30. Backing plates—for Electric, Hydraulic, Mechanical Brakes. Mechanical brake information was provided by AL-KO.

Electric

Hydraulic

Whether or not you will install brakes has to be decided before you purchase hubs, since the drums and hubs are inseparable and must be purchased as a unit. The brakes know to actuate when the appropriate signal initiates from the tow vehicle or nose of the trailer. Actuation at the trailer wheel occurs as a result of this signal which could be *hydraulic, electric or mechanical*. The apparatus you choose defines the type of system and actuation style.

Many state laws require trailers of certain weights or capacities to have brakes. In California, a trailer weight of more than 3000-lbs gross capacity or 1100-lbs empty requires brakes. It is a good idea to check your own state laws for their limits. Beyond the law, other considerations may influence your decision to install brakes. A smaller tow-car, an extra large motorhome or a tow vehicle of marginal braking capability should influence you to insist on some kind of trailer brakes. Rental trailers of almost all sizes use surge hydraulic brakes to give renters some form of braking. On the other hand, an extra large vehicle (in comparison to the trailer) with little or no cargo and with very good brakes will have a respectable amount of control over its tag-a-long. Unfortunately, for whatever reason, many trailers needing brakes—large as well as small—are without them.

Brakes—Electric

Electric brakes are a compromise of other systems with many advantages and only a few disadvantages. These brakes never operate off the forward inertia of the trailer as do hydraulic or mechanical. They are always controlled directly by action of the tow vehicle's driver. This independent control can be of great importance in a number of emergency situations, including sway where a little pull from the rear can help to straighten out the whole rig. Operation of these brakes requires the tow vehicle's electrical system for actuation. Several types of *brake controllers* are available which are installed in the tow vehicle for this purpose. These can be foot or handle controlled, triggered by either hydraulic pressure or brake light voltage. All controllers operate electric brakes by sending current to special backing plates which are fitted with electromagnets. The brake drum incorporates an armature plate. When current flows into the electromagnet, the armature plate attracts the magnet, which is then dragged thereby opening the shoes onto the drum, creating the necessary friction and a slowing of the rotation.

The amount of current sent by the controller can be varied. In some instances this is important since excessive current may cause the brakes to lock. This is usually due to a lighter gross (or total) trailer weight than the

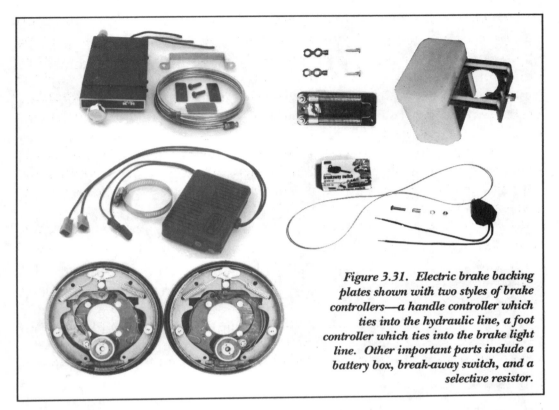

Figure 3.31. Electric brake backing plates shown with two styles of brake controllers—a handle controller which ties into the hydraulic line, a foot controller which ties into the brake light line. Other important parts include a battery box, break-away switch, and a selective resistor.

brake's design load. Adjustments are possible from the controller by twisting the handle. If more adjustment or reduction is needed, a **selective resistor** shown in Figure 3.31 can be installed. These resistors block and reduce the current flow to the brakes thereby eliminating brake locking due to a trailer weight that is too light.

Figure 3.31 shows several other items required for complete electric brake operation. Besides the basics—backing plates, armature plate and controller—break-away "accessories" are used to operate the brakes in event of a separation from the tow-car. The **six-volt battery,** its **box** and **break-away switch** are installed on the trailer near the coupler. The battery must be checked for juice often, since it will not operate the brakes if the battery is low or dead. The current must be constantly ready to flow through the switch to immediately apply the brakes, if the pin is pulled during a break-away.

Brakes—Hydraulic

Hydraulic brakes do not use any form of electricity and are much like the ones on your automobile. Hydraulic fluid is compressed through a tubular line which actuates a cylinder on the backing plate that then expands the brake shoes. The initiation of fluid flow through the

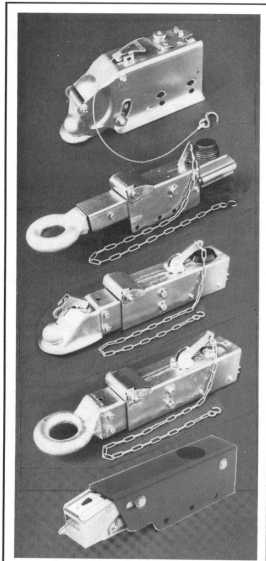

Figure 3.32. Five surge actuator/couplers from 6000 to 10,000-lb capacity.

brake lines to the brakes can be accomplished by either an actuator or a special attachment to the tow vehicle hydraulic brake lines. The first method requires installation of a special coupler called a surge actuator. Figure 3.32 shows several of these devices while Figure 3.33 and 3.34 show the hardware and brake line kit required to connect the two.

The *actuator/coupler* is welded to the nose of the trailer in place of the standard coupler. This specialized part contains a ball cup like most couplers which is part of a sliding mechanism. With one end attached to the tow vehicle, the other end of this sliding member is attached to the plunger of the *master cylinder* for the hydraulic trailer brakes. When the tow vehicle slows, stops or travels downhill, the trailer pushes forward, as the sliding mechanism is then pushed rearward. The resulting compression of the master cylinder pushes fluid through the hydraulic lines to the brakes at the wheels. The brake backing plates, mounted to the axles, have their own small cylinders which are moved by the compressed fluid. These cylinders open the brake shoes thereby applying the brakes. The ability to confine this system to the trailer alone encourages its use on trailers where different tow vehicles are to be used. Hence most rental yards choose this style over electric brakes. Boat trailers that are continually backed into the water prefer hydraulic brakes which are less susceptible to rust than electric brakes. Rust is not conducive to electrical conduction and can render the electric brakes inoperative.

The surge/hydraulic system is, however, not without disadvantages. Some of the problems encountered are *1)* on steep downgrades, the brakes can be on all the time causing them to overheat and fade; and *2)* a normal

Figure 3.33. Hydraulic brake backing plates shown here with hub & drum assembly. The bearing set includes a grease seal, dust cap & nuts as also part of the package. Actuator/ coupler (shown below) is usually sold separately, as is the hardware kit for complete installation.

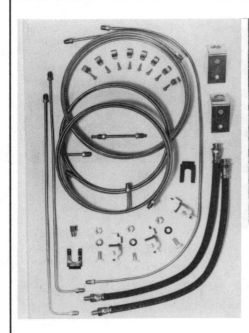

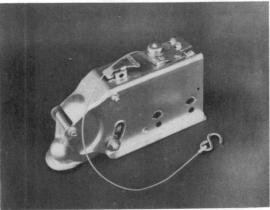

Figure 3.34. Hardware and brake line kit includes all the parts necessary for connecting hydraulic brakes at the hubs to the surge actuator at the coupler. An Atwood surge actuator is shown above.

brake application with a heavy trailer may result in violent "bucking" or "surging"; *3)* in the event of a sudden advanced trailer instability, surge brakes provide little help in restoring calm. However, in first heading downhill, these brakes may be helpful in keeping the rig below the critical speed where sway can begin. ***TRAILERS—How to Tow and Maintain*** describes these potential problems in more detail, and troubleshoots remedies.

In the past special connectors have been rigged to the tow vehicle's hydraulic brake lines. This eliminates the surge actuator and more effectively integrates the trailer braking system with that of the tow vehicle.

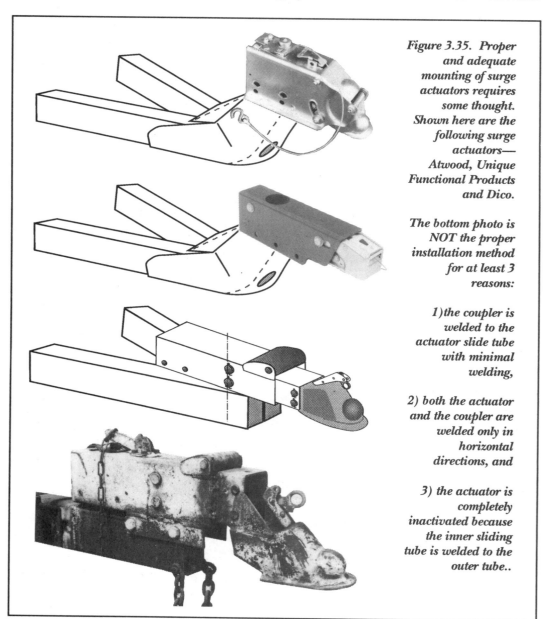

Figure 3.35. Proper and adequate mounting of surge actuators requires some thought. Shown here are the following surge actuators— Atwood, Unique Functional Products and Dico.

The bottom photo is NOT the proper installation method for at least 3 reasons:

1) the coupler is welded to the actuator slide tube with minimal welding,

2) both the actuator and the coupler are welded only in horizontal directions, and

3) the actuator is completely inactivated because the inner sliding tube is welded to the outer tube..

However, there is some amount of risk that improper installation could cause disruption or failing of the tow vehicle's braking system. Because of this along with greater expense and disapproval from auto manufacturers this method has never received wide acceptance.

Attachment of these surge actuator/couplers to the trailer is an area where attention is important. Several examples are shown in Figure 3.35. The first coupler shown here is manufactured by *Atwood* and is admirable in several ways. The loads have apparently been carefully evaluated during the design process. This coupler easily fits over 3-inch material, a very common size at the trailer nose. Angled tongue legs can also be specially mitered and welded to the sides of the coupler body at any angle according to the included instructions. In addition, the forward motion of the trailer rocks the coupling portion around a heavy duty pin joint which is positioned for easy detection of wear or damage. The mounting feature on the second coupler is also well designed, as is its smooth nose area. The third actuator is fabricated from two large pieces of tubing which slide one inside the other. There is no simple provision for slipping the coupler over the top of a frame member on the nose of the trailer. This coupler has to be laid on top of the trailer tongue and welded in place. Without reinforcement, the two short welds holding the coupler are then subjected to pealing loads, which are discussed in **Volume 2**. Pealing loads cause a higher stress level at the pealing corner, making it difficult to calculate the actual load and prepare the area properly. Hopefully the result is not as shown in the fourth illustration where the entire surge actuator is fully disabled with an over zealous welder. With the high rating of these couplers, provision for heavy duty mounting methods are a decided advantage and when not part of the design must be otherwise compensated.

Brakes—Mechanical

Mechanical brakes are a third style which are used almost exclusively in Europe. A few trailers using this system have recently been imported to the U.S. These brakes operate much like those used on older automobiles. Figure 3.36 illustrates the mechanics of the system. It is basically a surge or inertia style of brake at the coupler, relying on compression forces between trailer and tow-car for actuation. According to technical information received from *AL-KO*, a **brake rod** connects to the **compensator** which transfers the longitudinal motion into horizontal motion through the **Bowdry cable**. As this cable is pulled, one shoe is pushed against the drum which in turn activates the second shoe and the friction from the two then acts to slow the rotation. Exposure of cables to the elements can eventually result in some dragging and a less responsive

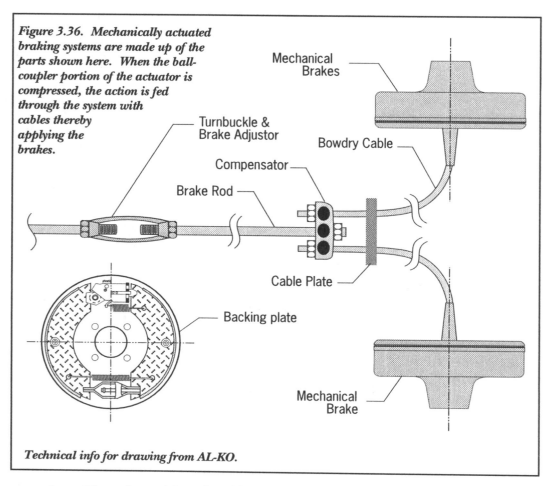

Figure 3.36. Mechanically actuated braking systems are made up of the parts shown here. When the ball-coupler portion of the actuator is compressed, the action is fed through the system with cables thereby applying the brakes.

Mechanical Brakes

Turnbuckle & Brake Adjustor

Bowdry Cable

Compensator

Brake Rod

Cable Plate

Backing plate

Mechanical Brake

Technical info for drawing from AL-KO.

stopping. Thus the cables should be checked and cleaned often to ensure a reliable braking system. One might want to note that the automotive industry abandoned mechanical brakes many years ago in favor of hydraulic brakes which have proven themselves to provide more efficient braking. In general, though, other than the disadvantages associated with any surge system, this style of brake is clean and trim while being easy to inspect and maintain. Europeans also seem to feel this braking system is superior since it is purely mechanical and there is no fluid to "top up." Also, due to its mechanical aspects, mechanical braking systems have relatively long term reliability, even if their efficiency is not as great.

CHAPTER 4.

BASIC COMPONENTS

With an enlightenment on suspensions and all the associated parts, we can now move onto smaller but no less important components. Once we have built the frame as discussed here and in **Volume 2** and added our suspension system, we will find the trailer can be loaded and its wheels will roll. However, to physically pull it with our tow vehicle we need to add a coupler, the first topic of discussion in this chapter. In addition, to be used legally on public roads, an electrical system with lights and wiring is required along with a license plate and a serial number. Fenders, as well as protection for your cargo and part of that finished look for your trailer, may also be part of the requirements to legalize it. These items, which form the next layer of important components, are discussed in this chapter.

A. COUPLERS

The **coupler** on the trailer fits over the **ball** on the **hitch** which is permanently attached to the tow vehicle. The coupler (Figures 4.1 to 4.3) is often incorrectly referred to as a hitch and clarification is usually in order for most conversations. Couplers, like hitches, are manufactured in four weight classifications, generally accepted as standard today, which are:

Class I	2000 lb. gross	Figure 4.4
Class II	3500 lb. gross	Figure 4.4
Class III	5000 lb. gross	Figure 4.5
Class IV	8500 lb. gross	Figure 4.6

The gross weight must include the trailer itself AND its cargo. For extremely heavy duty applications—over 8500 lb—few ball and coupler connections are strong enough. A **lunette eye**, Figure 4.5, should be used with the **pintle hook** shown in Figure 4.6. Whatever your application, it is important to know the eventual gross load and the coupler's stated rating.

The coupler or lunette eye must be securely attached to the tongue. This can be accomplished in a variety of ways. Couplers are available to fit angled or straight tongues. The 50° angle which accommodates a triangular or V-tongue is available in all capacities. Remember that I have found this angle to encourage tongues shorter than appropriate for the best towing configuration, as discussed in Chapter 2. But since little else is available, adjustments should be made. In my opinion, a coupler with a shallower angle (say 40°) would make it easier to build a long tongued trailer. Couplers with straight slots of 2-in channel width and 3-in width are designed to fit a straight tongue of channel or tubing of that size. A built up piece of material can also be used. Some of these couplers slide onto the

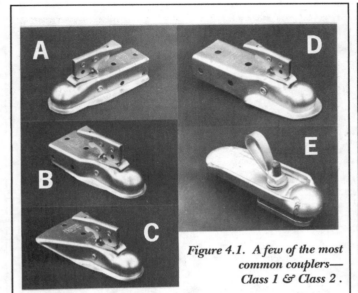

Figure 4.1. A few of the most common couplers—Class 1 & Class 2 .

No	Class	Style	Mfgr* Code
A	1	2" Channel	DL
B	1	3" Channel	DL
C	1	50° A-Frame	DL
D	2	3" Channel	AT
E	2	Universal Rental	DO
F	3	3" Channel	DL
G	3	2" Channel	AT
H	3	3" Channel	HB
I	3	3" Channel	UF
J	3	50° A-Frame	AT
K	3	50° A-Frame	HB
L	3	50° A-Frame	UF
M	4	3" Channel	AT
N	4	50° A-Frame	AT

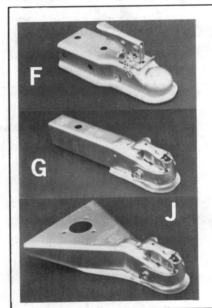

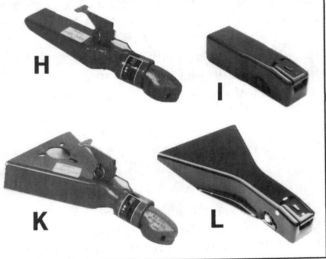

Figure 4.2. Class 3 couplers with 3-in channel, 2-in channel and 50° angle attachment provisions.

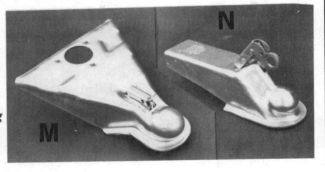

Figure 4.3. Class 4 couplers with 50° and 3-in channel mounting areas.

*Codes for manufacturer abbreviations used with the above are as follows:

AT	Atwood
DL	DuttonLainson
DO	Dolly
HB	Hammerblow
UF	Unique Functional Products

Basic Components

Figure 4.4. Trailer balls of various heights.

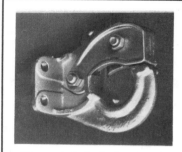

Figure 4.5. A pintle hook, for extra heavy duty towing.

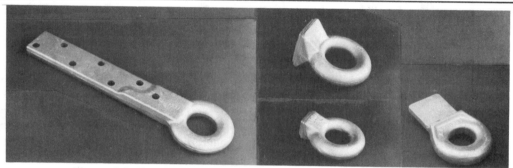

Figure 4.6. Lunette eyes with a variety of mounting configurations.

tongue from underneath, others from above. Three inch channel couplers fit the 40° *Step Neck*™, also mentioned in Chapter 2. A coupler used by many rental yards which is reportedly designed to fit a variety of ball sizes, is pictured as E in Figure 4.1.

There is a large assortment of couplers on the market—those shown here are only a few. How the coupler attaches to the tongue can affect the height of the trailer, which in turn may influence not only your choice of coupler but also your choice of axle; hence, the trailer's center of gravity and ultimately the trailer's performance. Don't treat this choice lightly. Chapter 2 discusses the attachment of couplers and the results and should be understood before you make a final selection of coupler. Selecting a coupler of adequate capacity and configuring the trailer to provide the highest performance will repay you in many miles of pleasant towing.

B. FENDERS

Although their primary purpose is to deflect debris and water thrown off by the tires, **fenders** greatly improve the looks of any trailer. They also often serve as a handy seat or platform. Fenders are not generally regulated by law but some states do require them under certain circumstances. In

California, a gross weight (trailer plus cargo) of 1500-lbs or more requires a trailer to be equipped with fenders. Many trailers below this weight are seen without fenders . . . as could be expected. *Fenders* are made in a variety of shapes and sizes but can be categorized as either t*rapezoidal, rolled, bent, half rolled or special formed*. Figure 4.7 illustrates some of the more common types available.

Finding a fender to fit over the tire may sound easy, but like everything else, a few traps can turn simplicity into frustration. The biggest challenge in selecting fenders is finding the style, shape and size to fit properly over the tire. The answer is not always as easy as it looks. The diameter of the tire must be known along with the height of the fender mounts. Most moderate size 14-in and 15-in wheels and tires will fit a fender 33-in across the bottom. Single axle fenders of this size are commonly roll-formed from a piece of metal which stretches out to a length

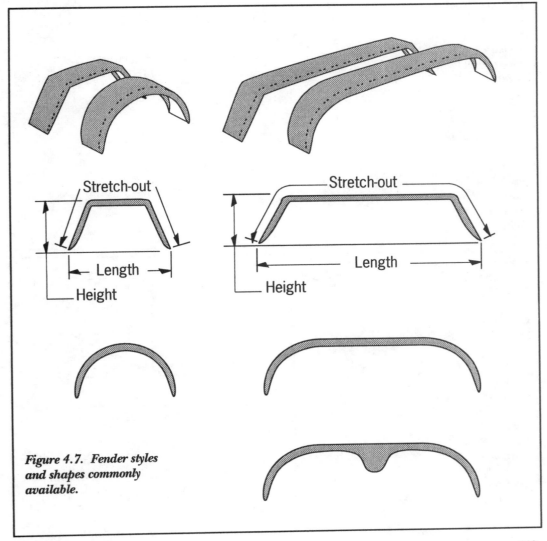

Figure 4.7. Fender styles and shapes commonly available.

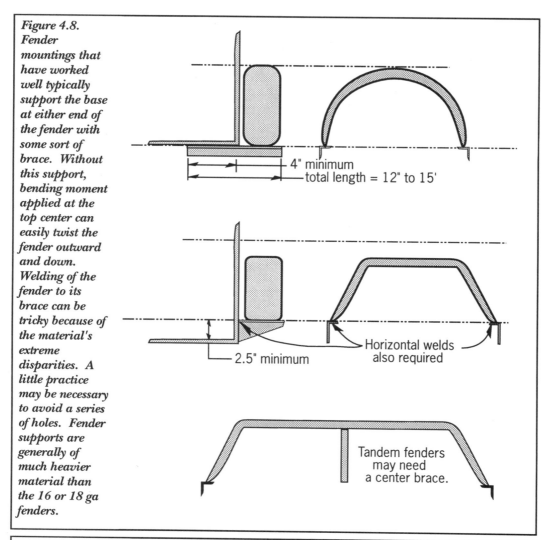

Figure 4.8. Fender mountings that have worked well typically support the base at either end of the fender with some sort of brace. Without this support, bending moment applied at the top center can easily twist the fender outward and down. Welding of the fender to its brace can be tricky because of the material's extreme disparities. A little practice may be necessary to avoid a series of holes. Fender supports are generally of much heavier material than the 16 or 18 ga fenders.

4" minimum
total length = 12" to 15'

2.5" minimum

Horizontal welds also required

Tandem fenders may need a center brace.

Figure 4.9. Fender mountings that have NOT worked well typically support the top or bottom from the side only. Anything that supports the top and lets the bottom flop, lets it do just that. Although the fender weight is light, bending loads applied at the top easily twist the methods shown.

of 44-in to 48-in long, and are rolled to finish widths of 6-in, 7-1/2-in or 9-in. A fender to fit a 14-in wheel may then be designated as a 7-1/2-in x 44-in x 33-in (width x stretch-out x length across the opening).

The final fender height will be determined by the position at which your fender braces are mounted. Some thought should be given to this while you're still drawing and certainly before you weld them in place. Figure 4.8 shows a few examples of fender mountings I have found to work well for me, while 4.9 shows a few that haven't worked well.

Fender clearance problems are often just as difficult to sort out;

A. Unloaded trailer—note straight axle. Sometimes axles are precambered with a center bend to give the wheels a positive camber.

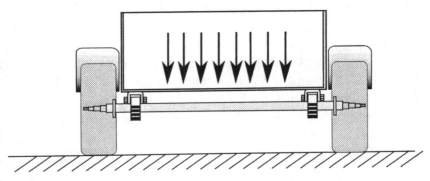

B. Loaded trailer—note negative camber of wheels

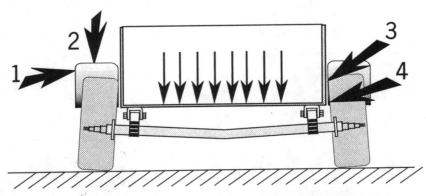

Figure 4.10. Axles are typically "positive cambered" in the center to accommodate the addition of basic weight which generally brings the wheels and tires close to vertical. Additional loads can then bend the axle as shown in B. This puts the top of the wheel/tire closer to the trailer frame and the upper fender down closer to the tire. These changes must be accounted for when fenders are installed. Clearance problem areas to check:

1) Edge of fender/tire tread,
2) Top of tire/underside of fender,
3) Body side/inside sidewall of tire,
4) Tire tread/fender brace.

sometimes more so since the tire moves in unexpected directions not just up and down. The actual movement of the tire in relation to the fender depends mostly on the suspension style and how it is mounted. A standard style spring with shackles in the back will move the tire slightly back as it also moves up; with shackles in the front, it will move forward and up. A torsion suspension will also move both directions following the circumference of its circle (usually back and up). This slight movement must be accounted for when defining the fender clearance required. The rear (or front) fender brace may need to be moved rearward (or forward) to accommodate the slight horizontal movement.

Figure 4.10 illustrates other common problems. First of all, the clearance from the top of the tire to the underside of the fender *(point #2)* must be sufficient to allow a fender to clear the tire when a bump is encountered. A commonly used dimension for this is 3 to 4 inches or about a fist height. Fender braces must be set to provide this clearance. Secondly, the inside top of the tire moves inward toward the frame as the load increases. This is called a negative camber on the wheels. When a bump is hit, this movement is even greater. At least 1/2 to 3/4-inch should be provided for this clearance *(point #3 & #4)*.

Finally, fender width must be enough to cover the tread of the tire *(point #1)* and not cut its edge down through the tire tread or sidewall. In severe cases of inside tire interference, wheel spacers, Figure 4.12, can be used to increase the offset dimension by about 5/16-in. In some cases to ensure full thread engagement of the lug nut, the use of longer studs may be required. A choice of different wheels with an offset further to the outside are also a possibility. Remember though that too much offset can create

Figure 4.11. Fender with potential clearance problems. Unless this trailer has an unsprung axle, a small bump will easily put the fender down on top of the tire tread.

Figure 4.12. To gain additional clearance from the inner wall, wheel spacers can be used for spacing a wheel out from the trailer body. Be careful here, too much spacing can weaken the attachment.

interference problems with the outside fender flange—and impose excessive wear on the bearings.

The tire and fender shown in Figure 4.11 is an example of a clearance far too close for my comfort. If this is not an unsprung trailer, this tire is in for some rough treatment. Even if it is unsprung, at 60 mph the tread on a tire can grow up to an inch in diameter causing interference with the underside of the fender. With the tire's existing negative camber and the body roll from bumps, the outer fender edge is poised to cut the sidewall.

C. ELECTRICAL SYSTEM

Equally, if not more important, is the delineation of your trailer with lights. Driving at night, abiding by the law or indicating braking to the fellow behind you—all require lights on your trailer . . . just like on your automobile. Lights are mounted on the frame: wires are connected to them and to a pigtail or plug at the very front of the trailer. The power to operate this system is drawn from your tow-car's 12-volt battery. In many ways, it is all quite simple—a mere extension of the principle system used in your automobile. In other ways the electrical system can be quite complex with all its minute parts and pieces . . . and especially baffling, if it doesn't work.

To demonstrate the workings of this system, one trailer lamp can be used as shown in Figure 4.13. The trailer must be connected (and thereby grounded) to the tow vehicle during this test. A helper will simplify this experiment. Find the tow car brake light wire and connect a wire between it and the loose lamp. Have your friend depress the brake pedal. The lamp does not light. Now, with the brake pedal depressed, touch the metal body of the loose lamp to the body of the trailer. Assuming you have done everything correctly (and you are touching bare metal, not paint) the lamp should light up. Figure 4.13 illustrates the method of connection required for this experiment. (The clearance light/headlight circuit could also be used and no helper would be required, as the headlight switch can be turned on and left on. Don't forget to turn it off when you're done, though.)

Each trailer lamp is connected in this manner to the corresponding lamp in the tow vehicle and grounded through the trailer's metal body. Electric brakes require the same type of connection; i.e. a ground to the trailer frame and a wire connected to an on-off switch, usually in the form of an electric brake controller.

That's the basic theory. How about the real thing? What happens when you go to buy lights? Wire? How do you mount them? Where? Too often this system is not given the importance it deserves, and the placement of lights is delayed to the last phase of the project. This sequence of events generally follows a pattern . . .

> figure out and buy the suspension . . .
> layout and build the frame . . .
> attach the suspension . . .
> set the trailer up on its wheels and
> then stand back and say "I'm done" . . .

And in the same breath, as you notice the lack thereof, you gasp . . . "Uh oh! Where do I put the lights? and run the wire?" By now this question has become a serious problem. In fact, it is going to require such a staggering amount of work to weld wire guides from awkward positions, drill the necessary holes from weird angles and generally work in, around, and under your trailer that the question of feasibility may be purely academic . . . but this step must be done, or you won't have lights. Licensing the trailer and driving at night will be impossible; day driving very unwise.

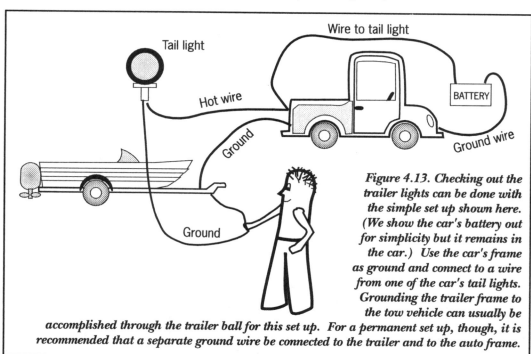

Tail light

Wire to tail light

Hot wire

BATTERY

Ground

Ground wire

Ground

Figure 4.13. Checking out the trailer lights can be done with the simple set up shown here. (We show the car's battery out for simplicity but it remains in the car.) Use the car's frame as ground and connect to a wire from one of the car's tail lights. Grounding the trailer frame to the tow vehicle can usually be accomplished through the trailer ball for this set up. For a permanent set up, though, it is recommended that a separate ground wire be connected to the trailer and to the auto frame.

To avoid this scenario, the time to think about the electrical system is first! Up front! Before you cut metal! At least before you weld it! This process can be handled toward the end of your geometric layout if you have followed the suggested steps and done a drawing. The best approach is to interweave it with the whole design process. Certainly you want to determine it before you start to layout and weld your framework. And if holes need to be drilled or torched it can be done before you cover them up. Sufficient, timely attention to this area will save you time, money and a lot of headaches.

D. ELECTRICAL—LIGHTING

There are three hardware parts to any trailer's electrical system—lights, wire, connectors. Lights are the most obvious and are most often thought of first. Lights themselves can be quite confusing because of all the available mounting methods and the huge variety of styles. In addition, prices don't seem to be particularly consistent with quality. Sorting out these variables can become quite a project. After we discuss lights, we will talk a little about the options for mounting them.

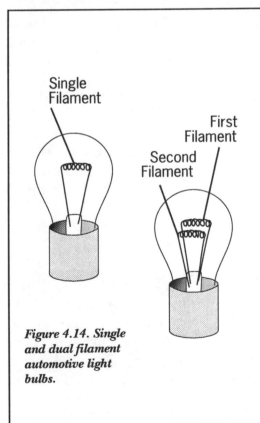

Single Filament

First Filament

Second Filament

Figure 4.14. Single and dual filament automotive light bulbs.

Electrical—Lights

Lights, themselves consist of a housing, a bulb and a wire pigtail for connecting to the main trailer wiring harness. Some lights have 2 wires which means the bulb used with the light has 2 filaments, as shown in Figure 4.14. Each filament itself requires only one wire because the other half of the circuit is the ground, which moves through the housing onto the trailer frame. Plastic lights have to have special attachments incorporated into the light to provide for a ground. The bulb in most tail lights has 2 filaments. Just like most American cars, the brake light filament is the same as the turn signal filament,

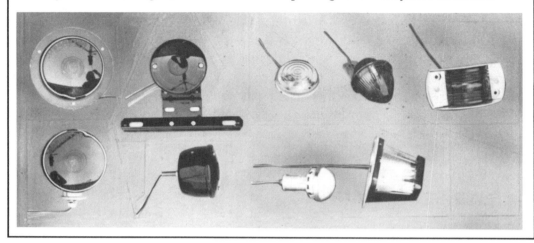

Figure 4.15. Tail lights, clearance and license plate lights commonly used on trailers.

while the clearance light filament is on a completely separate circuit. Most foreign cars these days have separate turn signal and brake light circuits. The two systems cannot be directly connected without an adapter. Lamps have several functions on a trailer. They are used for

> tail lights,
> clearance & marker lights,
> turn signals—both right and left,
> license plate illumination,
> braking lights.

If you have a travel, horse or covered trailer, lighting for the interior will be a consideration and back-up lights are also a nice feature. Figure 4.15 shows several styles of lamps currently available and commonly used on trailers. Once you begin to research lights, you may feel a bit overwhelmed by the number of choices. Lights can be purchased for just about every conceivable purpose. There are numerous manufacturers with a wide range of quality and pricing.

Electrical—Mounting & the Law

In addition to hardware, there are two areas involving the trailer's electrical system which might be considered "software"—mounting and the laws. Since many laws dictate where to place lights, these subjects go hand in hand. To respect and comply with the various laws of your state, attention to mounting of lights is crucial. While some consumers refuse to pay more for something that does not directly increase the fun—lights, in this case; most of us want our trailers to be seen at night and can appreciate that being without lights may well decrease the "fun" instead! It is certainly easy to appreciate good lights on the vehicle in front of you; and if your trailer lights do the job, the person behind you will be appreciative, too. In general, most vehicle lighting laws require:

1) delineation of length, width and excessive height
   with clearance lights and tail lights;
2) delineation of same with reflectors to enhance the
   lighting and provide a bright spot in the event of
   a burned out light;
3) separate turn signal lamps on the appropriate side;
4) rear lights to indicate braking; and
5) a license plate illuminator.

In California, all lights must be clearly visible from 300-feet. Your state's laws may vary from this and should be checked. In many states every light from a manufacturer must pass rigid tests regarding its illumination and construction, before even being offered for sale. Assuming it passes, a certificate to sell that light must be purchased and kept on file in a state office. Quite a rigamarole for just a light. But lights are important and for consumer assurance these regulations are also important.

Mounting locations should be chosen for maximum visibility, protection, economy and durability. The precise placement on your framework is up to you. There is no law that states how many screws or nuts or hooks or welds must be used to attach the light. If anything at all, the law may state "secure attachment," leaving the details to you. Each light will have its own special mounting arrangement and requirement. Before you purchase any lights, consider seriously the method you plan to use to mount them. The mounting of lights has several constraints, many of which can become conflicting:

1) lights must be easily visible and delineate the size of the
   vehicle—both length and width;
2) lights must be positioned to resist being knocked off easily;
3) the brackets must be designed to resist vibration failure;
4) mounting with available tools must be possible;
5) local Motor Vehicle Departments and police must approve.

Item 1) and 5) are quite commonly in conflict with items 2), 3), 4). For example, mounting of lights for visibility, 1), is easy if the lights protrude crudely from the trailer sides. This approach generally conflicts with items 2) and 3) where knockoff is easy and vibration resistance poor. For a travel or covered trailer, lights can easily be mounted on the extreme corners. For a utility, horse or boat trailer where the bed drops down between the wheels and tires, mounting of lights can become a real challenge.

Other important considerations include the bouncing from road bumps, which can be severe and should not be underestimated. Bear in mind that lights are quite light in weight and thus do not need a heavy weight bracket to support them. This, however, can be deceiving. A heavier bracket improperly connected frequently accentuates vibration problems and hastens a new crack, a new break. But a bracket too light, especially with a heavier weight at the end can also break easily. In my experience, mounting of lights can be a real challenge. Thinking about the mounting method and designing this in advance makes the final assembly process much easier.

E. ELECTRICAL—WIRING

Although painting (Chapter 6) should precede installation of final wiring, it will be discussed here since procurement and preparation for it must be done prior to painting. However, a quick look at the end of Chapter 6 will help you coordinate the two activities. Your method of wiring should be planned in advance—wire guides placed, brackets for mounting of lights positioned and installed, holes for attachment of lights and ground wire holes drilled.

Wire used on trailers is not the same as that used in your home. Building construction wire is single strand and must carry 110 volts AC (alternating current). The wire used in your automobile and subsequently your trailer must be "stranded", i.e. several tiny strands of wire are wound together building up to the size of wire designated. It is designed to carry 12 volts DC (direct current). The actual wire size is an important consideration. For tail, clearance and turn signal lights, a 16 or 18 gauge size is usually adequate. Electric brakes draw a lot of current and 14 gauge is a minimum choice for effective operation and safety. Wire too small may overheat, short out or start a fire, while wire too large is expensive and wasted copper.

Wires should be protected from the elements as much as possible and from the hard to avoid sharp corners found on most trailers. Notched or brittle wires short circuit easily. One option is to run conduit the full length of your trailer. In my experience, the expense and difficulty of installation make conduit a less than desirable choice. If the tongue and frame are tubing, a handy built-in form of conduit already exists. Any intermediate connector holes should be torched, not drilled, to reduce sharp edges. Although rubber grommets can be used in drilled holes, finding the right diameter and thickness is often difficult. Once found, though, retaining the grommet in place can be accomplished with weatherstrip adhesive. Another choice is the use of wires shrouded in a secondary plastic jacket—an inexpensive protection without the hassle of conduit. A single layer of coating embrittles, splits and renders the wires susceptible to shorts more rapidly than secondarily coated wires. A cross section of such a *jacketed wire* is shown in Figure 4.16. Single wires without this secondary jacket should be avoided on a trailer wherever possible.

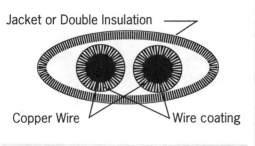

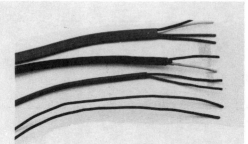

Figure 4.16. A typical cross section of jacketed electrical wire is shown above. The two inner wires are usually of two different colors: either **black and red** *or* **black and white**. *Actual jacketed wire is also shown with 4 inner wires and with 2 inner wires.*

Routing wires and connecting lights to the plug at the coupler can be done a number of ways, as shown in Figures 4.17 through 4.19. Wires can be placed down one side of the trailer with smaller wires stretched across the back of the frame to the other side, as in Figure 4.17. This method works well for narrower trailers without clearance lights. Wires can also be drawn down both sides with extensor single strand wires pulled a short distance to clearance lights, if used, as in Figure 4.18. In California, these two methods could be used with trailers under 80-inch width. Figure 4.19 is the method used when electric brakes and clearance lights are added—ostensibly for trailers over 80-inches wide.

Color coding of wires is another consideration which simplifies tracing of wire functions, especially important when shorts or problems occur. This simple procedure assigns a different color of wire for each light function. The chosen color then runs from the connector to the light itself. Colors commonly used on trailers are shown in Figure 4.20. A sampling of automobile color codes, shown here also, indicates that colors vary considerably from one vehicle manufacturer to the next. The automobile's wide array of systems — windows, air conditioning, radio, warning lights — which a trailer does not have dictates complex color codes which seem to call for the choice of black and/or white ground wires. Other considerations take precedence for a trailer.

Through the years, trade customs have evoked the use of certain

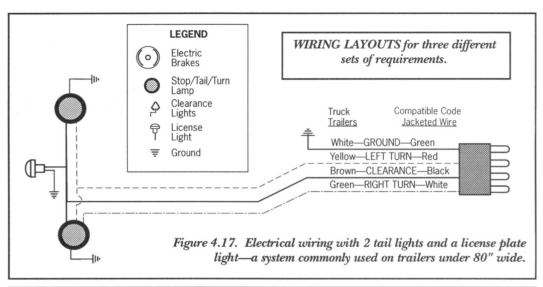

Figure 4.17. *Electrical wiring with 2 tail lights and a license plate light—a system commonly used on trailers under 80" wide.*

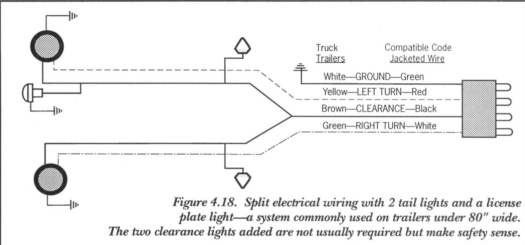

Figure 4.18. *Split electrical wiring with 2 tail lights and a license plate light—a system commonly used on trailers under 80" wide. The two clearance lights added are not usually required but make safety sense.*

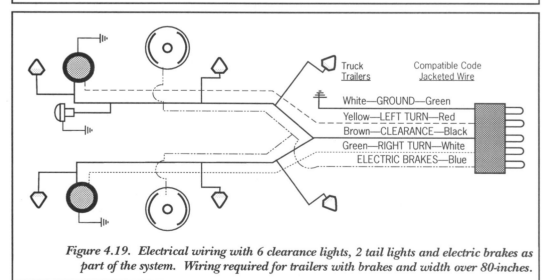

Figure 4.19. *Electrical wiring with 6 clearance lights, 2 tail lights and electric brakes as part of the system. Wiring required for trailers with brakes and width over 80-inches.*

Figure 4.20. Various wiring codes used on trailers and automobiles.

TRAILER Codes:

	Compatible Code Jacketed Wire	Truck Trailers
Ground	Green	White
Left Turn/Stop	Red	Yellow
Right Turn/Stop	White	Green
Clearance	Black	Brown
Electric Brakes	Yellow or Blue	
Interior	Blue or Yellow	
Left Tail	Black/Red	
Right Tail	Black/White	

TRAILER Wiring Colors (*used in ENGLAND*[11])

Ground or Earth	White
Left Turn	Yellow
Right Turn	Green
Interior	Blue
Electric Brakes	——No color specified
Clearance	——(Replaced by the next 3)
Stop	Red
Left Side Tail	Black
Right Side Tail	Brown

AUTO Wire Colors:	**Chevy Trucks & Vans**[19]		**AMC**[20]	**Toyota**[21]
Ground	Black	Black	Black	White/Black
Left Turn Signal	Dk Green	Yellow	Lt Green w/ TR	Green/Black
Right Turn Signal	Dk Green	Dk Green	Lt Green	Green/Yellow
Brake Light	_____	_____	_____	Green/White
Clearance	Brown	Brown	White	Green

color codings which, as it turns out, actually conflict with market avail-ability of products to produce the best result, especially for small trailer manufacturers and individuals. *Jacketed* wires, discussed earlier, are available as high volume manufactured items in "black/white" or "black/red" at affordable prices. A color coding to accommodate availability of this product, would make it easier to use this superior approach. As it is now, many manufacturers use a standardized code at the main pigtail to the tow vehicle, but use unjacketed black or whatever color they can get the rest of the way back. Without test equipment, it then becomes extremely difficult for end users to decipher which wire is which. The purpose of the color code is then defeated and shorts are next to impossible to trace.

On the other hand, the decision to adhere to a color code common to truck trailers often eliminates the superior solution—jacketed wires, since the proper colors are not easily available. Is there a solution to this dilemma? Wire manufacturers could provide jacketed wires in colors easily used with common practice such as brown/yellow and brown/green. Unfortunately, the trailer market is quite small and far too price sensitive for such an item to be sold at acceptable prices.

Another solution? Provide a more compatible color code, as suggested in Figure 4.20. The "Compatible Code" of recommended colors, in my opinion, combines the best of all possibilities. The colors are easy to remember— *white* is right, *green* is ground, *black* is basic for clearance, etc. Color coded jacketed wire is readily available without a special order. And being able to decipher which wire is which along with the protection afforded by jacketed wire keeps problems to a minimum. Currently, few trailers are fully color coded so changing to this easier code is not as difficult as it may first appear. Remember, there are no laws requiring that a specific color code be used anywhere (only suggestions), so the choice is entirely up to you.

F. ELECTRICAL—CONNECTIONS

Electrical connections include not only the individual connectors where two pieces of wire or more are connected but also the main plug at the front of the trailer that is used to connect the electrical system of the trailer to that of the tow vehicle. Since each has its important points, we will discuss each separately.

Electrical—Pigtails

The pigtail and receptacle at the trailer coupling can range from a simple and minimal four wire flat plug that hangs loose, to a seven prong round with bending protection spring. The *receptacle* is attached to the tow vehicle. It can hang loose or be bolted to the rear of the chassis or bodywork. Right now the quantity and designs of plugs and receptacles is phenomenal, not to mention the price ranges. It's hard to imagine such a simple product that can take on so many different configurations . . . but they do. Figure 4.21 illustrates a few of the more common varieties. The *plug* generally attaches to the trailer. Materials used on these plugs can be metal, plastic or a rubber compound.

My experience is that plugs with metal bodies short out after a period of time due to the rust that develops from being exposed to the elements. In addition assembly is difficult since hooking the wires over the necessarily tiny screws and tightening them can be tedious. This is a job best done with small hands. Alternatively, molded rubber plugs are easy to install and attach to tow vehicle wires: they have been known to resist the elements by

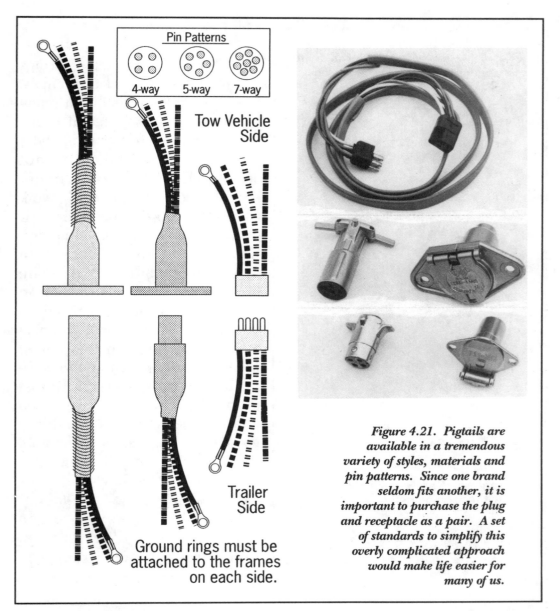

Pin Patterns

4-way   5-way   7-way

Tow Vehicle Side

Trailer Side

Ground rings must be attached to the frames on each side.

Figure 4.21. Pigtails are available in a tremendous variety of styles, materials and pin patterns. Since one brand seldom fits another, it is important to purchase the plug and receptacle as a pair. A set of standards to simplify this overly complicated approach would make life easier for many of us.

not shorting out (on me, anyway) for as long as 10 years. Because of the current complexities of such a simple product, I would like to suggest that a set of standardized connector dimensions be developed so all plugs, regardless of material, will fit all receptacles, just as they do in your home. With 10 million registered trailers in this country, one has to ask why this has not been done. The heavy duty trucking industry has standardized the plugs used on semi-trailers. Europeans have also standardized their plugs. The telephone industry has standardized its plugs and so has the computer industry. It seems a simple step for our recreational trailer industry to do this. I might suggest a 7-way that can be reduced to a 4 or 5-way with holes that will still fit the basic 7-way receptacle.

Electrical—Connectors

Tying wires together brings another set of special challenges. Connectors are available in many styles; some need special tools, some don't. The screw on style, requiring no tools, is not appropriate for use on a trailer because these can too easily work themselves loose. These connectors are designed for use in homes, which don't move except in earthquakes. Stripping the wire ends for a clean connection should be done as shown in Chapter 6. If you own a crimping tool, (as pictured in Chapter 6) *nylon closed end connectors* are probably the easiest and most practical. They cover the exposed ends of the wire and provide a good solid connection. Twisting the wires before crimping, also shown in Chapter 6, will help lock the wires in place. *Scotch-loks™* require only a pliers and are an excellent but bulkier choice. Although a bit more expensive,

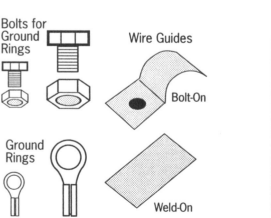

Figure 4.22. Connectors of various types can be used with success, but screw on styles for home building should be avoided. Wire guides which can be welded or bolted keep wires in place.

Nylon Closed End Connectors

Scotch Loks™

Removable

Longitudinal Crimp Style

Screw-on Style Not recommended for use on trailers

Bolts for Ground Rings

Wire Guides

Bolt-On

Ground Rings

Weld-On

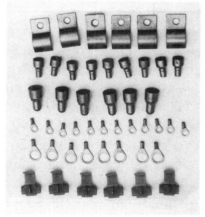

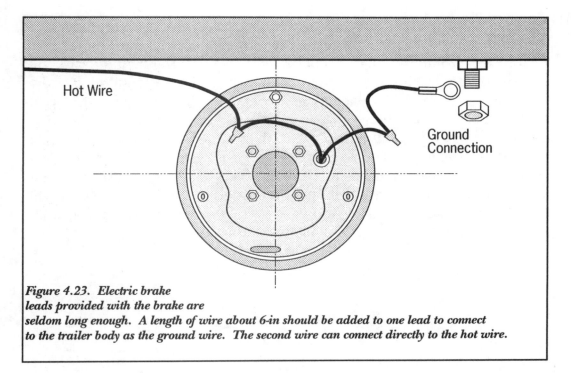

Hot Wire

Ground
Connection

*Figure 4.23. Electric brake
leads provided with the brake are
seldom long enough. A length of wire about 6-in should be added to one lead to connect
to the trailer body as the ground wire. The second wire can connect directly to the hot wire.*

they are also ideal for tapping into continuous wire you don't want to cut.
Disconnectable styles are available and necessary only for special cases;
besides the extra expense, water has been known to leak in, creating a bad
connection. Figure 4.22 illustrates some of the connectors from which you
have to choose.

To complete the circuit, **ground connectors** must be part of the
system. Ground connections require a little different approach but must not
be treated lightly. As you found in the earlier test, Figure 4.13, lights do not
work without a good ground connection. The consequence of a loose
ground is lights that work intermittently or worse, that work not at all. Most
flickering trailer lights can be traced to an inadequate ground. Each light
operates because the ground completes the circuit. Thus the connection
must be substantial and solid. Rusty mounting surfaces or lead wires bent
under the bulb can defeat this requirement. In your tow vehicle the ground
cable connects from the battery to a body panel or frame member. Each
and every light has one hot wire which connects to a passing wire while the
other side touches the frame. The same is true of the trailer—lights are
grounded through their mounting bolts; brakes with a wire bolted to the
frame. The ground connection between trailer and tow-car is very
important and should be accomplished with a wire connection rather than
through the ball-coupler attachment as was done in the test and as
attempted on many trailers. The small ground ring shown in Figure 4.22,
crimped to the wire, and bolted to the trailer frameworks well for this.

Electric brakes need 2 connections and are provided with 2 protruding wires for this purpose. A ground connector must be used on one of them, while the other is connected to a wire that extends to the front of the trailer and eventually connects to the brake controller in the tow vehicle. A ring or U-shape style connector works well over a bolt that has previously been welded to the framework. In this case a larger ring over a short larger bolt has advantages. My experience is that the pigtail out of standard backing plates never seems to be long enough for trailers I've worked on and usually needs to be lengthened by about 3-in to 6-in. Be sure to allow plenty of wire for suspension travel but not so much that it will get tangled. A properly connected trailer wiring system will serve you well. It is worth the effort to design it carefully and install it properly.

CHAPTER 5.

ACCESSORIES

A. Safety Devices

B. Accessories
- Trailer Jacks
- Caster Wheels & Jack Mountings
- Winches
- Tie Downs
- Anti-Theft

C. Fabricated Accessories
- Tool Boxes
- Stakesides
- Racks & Carriers

Accessories are primarily available to enhance your trailer's utility. Certain accessories make it considerably easier to just plain use your trailer. Others are safety oriented. Most trailer types—boat, horse, utility—have their own unique list of accessories. For instance, horse trailers offer saddle racks, tack hangers, feeder bins, double or single doors and windows. Boat trailers may offer extra rollers, tie downs or a heavy duty winch. Car haulers will offer tool boxes, longer ramps, tie downs and wheel-stops. Here we will discuss some items which are popular on a wide range of trailers and a few fabricated items which might have application to flatbeds, utility or maybe even boat trailers.

A. SAFETY DEVICES

Let's start with safety devices since all trailers are required to have some of these. These parts occupy a minority of spaces in the list of trailer accessories. They include *safety chains, coupler lock pins, break-away locking mechanisms* for electric and surge brakes and *tie downs.* The *break-away switch* for electric brakes, which is activated should the trailer become separated from its tow vehicle, was discussed in Chapter 3 in the section on brakes. Surge and mechanical brakes are also equipped with a break-away locking device in the form of a lever and a chain that hooks loosely to the tow vehicle. If the trailer breaks away, the chain is pulled activating the brake mechanism thereby applying the brakes. Tie down straps, along with stakesides and tailgates may also be considered a form of safety device since they act to hold everything in place which would otherwise not be held. We will discuss these shortly.

Safety chains are required on all trailers; even so, they

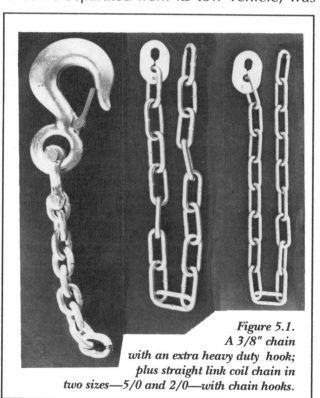

*Figure 5.1.
A 3/8" chain
with an extra heavy duty hook;
plus straight link coil chain in
two sizes—5/0 and 2/0—with chain hooks.*

PROOF COIL STEEL CHAIN —Grade 30						
Trade size		Minimum Material Diameter	Link ID	MAX Safe Lifting Load Lbs	Minimum Proof Test Load Lbs	Minimum Break Test Load Lbs
Inches	mm					
3/16	5	0.218	0.95	750	1500	3000
1/4	7	0.276	1.19	1250	2500	5000
5/16	8	0.315	1.27	1900	3800	7600
3/8	10	0.394	1.36	2650	5300	10600
1/2	13	0.519	1.72	4500	9000	18000
5/8	16	0.356	2.12	6900	13800	37600
3/4	20	0.718	2.65	9750	19500	39000

Data from **McMaster Carr Catalog**[10] & **Federal Specification**[13]

Figure 5.2. Chain strengths are given in tables such as the one shown here. Be sure you understand the meaning of each listed number before you select a chain. Remember that impact loads can easily double minimum requirements. MAXimum lifting load is also called Working Load Limit.

usually elicit a bit of controversy. Many owners say they'd rather the chain break and the trailer run loose if the trailer and tow vehicle separate. Others know the dire consequences of that scenario and the importance of the trailer staying with something steerable. Of course, if your tow vehicle is not sufficient in size to be towing the trailer in the first place, any mishap can be disastrous.

Whatever your opinion, most state laws require the use of safety chains. Chains need to be heavy enough to hold the trailer in place in the event of break-away. You may never need to use them, (and let's hope you don't), but if the chains won't withstand an impact load, they'll be useless in that once-in-a-lifetime event. Figure 5.1 shows a few examples of chains in common use. Strengths of chain are listed in Figure 5.2. A single chain can be figured to have the strength listed in the chart. Two chains or a loop of chain effectively doubles the load capability. A double set of chain loops quadruples it. Figure 5.3 illustrates these configurations. If the chain is used for lifting and moving, it will be subjected to "working loads." For this use, the *working load limit* given in most chain specification tables is vital to observe. With a trailer, though, the chain typically hangs loose waiting for that one emergency impact load. Here the load of interest is the *breaking strength* (Figure 5.2). However, using the *proof test load* provides a better margin of safety. The best advice is to be conservative and by all means query your supplier for the exact load rating.

The weakest link in a chain connection is often its attachment to the trailer, especially if the chain end is welded. Chains are not designed to be welded. As with springs, the careful preparation of alloys and heat treating is too easily undone by a weld. A U-loop or eye loop of heavier hot rolled or cold rolled bar 1/4-in to 3/8-in will not only give a good length of weld—3-inch to 6-inch—but also strength to match that of the chain. The damage to the chain links instilled by the welding process is thus avoided.

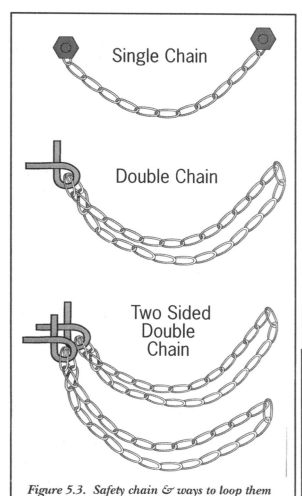

Single Chain

Double Chain

Two Sided
Double
Chain

Figure 5.3. Safety chain & ways to loop them using a loop or Ty-d-eye^tm welded to the trailer.

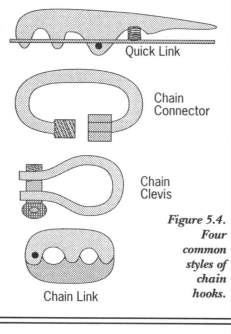

Quick Link

Chain
Connector

Chain
Clevis

*Figure 5.4.
Four
common
styles of
chain
hooks.*

Chain Link

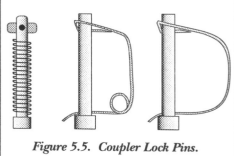

Figure 5.5. Coupler Lock Pins.

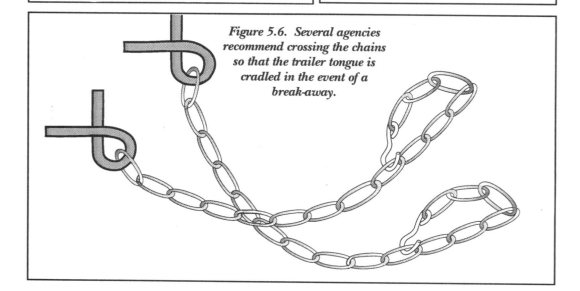

Figure 5.6. Several agencies recommend crossing the chains so that the trailer tongue is cradled in the event of a break-away.

Connecting the loose ends of chain together is another puzzle. Too often the solution is the most easily grabbed bolt and nut that will fit through the links—an unsatisfactory choice due to the potential lack of strength and inconvenience of use. Inexpensive devices shown in Figure 5.4 are generally referred to as **chain hooks** . These devices make it much easier and more reliable to connect the chain ends. Most are available in a variety of strengths. Just be sure to coordinate the strength of this part with that of your chain.

The **coupler lock pin** is another piece of hardware for safety, as well as convenience. It is designed to prevent accidental opening of the coupler latch. Too often, a nut and bolt is used—again, a less than desirable solution due mostly to the inherent weakness of the threaded shaft. A few lock pin styles are shown in Figure 5.5. Finding a pin like this with the correct diameter usually requires some searching, since few trailer companies carry them. A search of one or two specialty, well-equipped, hardware stores may be a better source and yield a find more quickly.

B. ACCESSORIES

Accessories are an integral part of your trailer and make the trailer do the job initially set out for it. **Basic accessories**, useful for all trailer's, include jacks, caster wheels, winches, tie downs and anti-theft devices. Fabricated and special accessories include tailgates, sidewalls, racks, bins and compartments, covers and any other accessories particularly suited to the trailer's end use. Basic accessories can usually be purchased outright, while many others must be fabricated from scratch. Besides the price of the components the availability of metal working equipment will probably be a factor in your decision to buy, sub-out or make. Jacks and caster wheels, winches, tie downs and some tool boxes can be purchased outright. Products such as these produced on a machine are often far superior to anything you could fabricate. If the styles you want are available, lots of time can also be saved.

Accessories—Trailer Jacks

Jacks are available in many styles for a wide variety of different specialized purposes. Jack names—tongue, stabilizer, swivel, side rack lift and extra heavy duty—can refer to placement on the trailer, type of cranking or purpose of use. Jacks can simplify and ease your working with a trailer. Figure 5.7 shows some of the different styles of jacks available.

The most common style of *jack* is mounted on the trailer tongue with a *caster wheel*, is called a *jockey wheel* or *tongue jack,* and facilitates moving the trailer when it is detached from the tow vehicle. In addition, raising and lowering the coupler into position for connecting and disconnecting to the ball on the tow vehicle is simplified. Using a jack mounted in this position also reduces the potential for back injuries or pinched fingers caused by attempts to lift a heavily loaded trailer tongue onto the tow-car's hitch ball. I would not own a trailer without one.

    Stabilizer jacks are used when equipment mounted to a trailer bed needs stabilizing while the trailer is stopped and the equipment is in operation. Some of the popular styles are shown in Figure 5.8 and 5.9. Almost any jack with a flat foot attached can act as a stabilizing agent. Many builders have resorted to a square (or round) tube which slides through a larger tube. To modify the height of this *drop leg jack*, two methods are used—a nut welded to the outer tube with a screw which tightens and holds the position with friction, or several position holes drilled through both tubings which accept a large pin. *Swivel jacks*, Figure 5.8, have also been a popular choice for this duty because of their strength, convenience and versatility. The swivel mount permits carrying the jack sideways leaving the area above the frame unobstructed for doors to swing open or loads to extend. The available variety of configurations—top wind or side wind, frame or tube swivel mount, a multitude of overall heights and extensions, capacities of 1000-lbs to 5000-lbs, a choice of jack foot or caster wheel—make this style of jack a versatile accessory.

    Swing-up, hide-away jacks, Figure 5.9, are also used for stabilizing

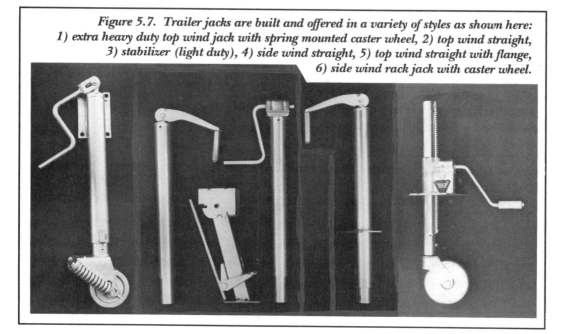

Figure 5.7. Trailer jacks are built and offered in a variety of styles as shown here: 1) extra heavy duty top wind jack with spring mounted caster wheel, 2) top wind straight, 3) stabilizer (light duty), 4) side wind straight, 5) top wind straight with flange, 6) side wind rack jack with caster wheel.

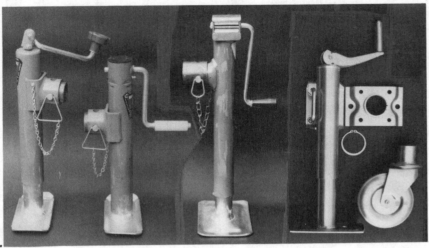

Figure 5.8. Three Hammerblow swivel jacks— 1 top wind & 2 side wind— with tube mounts. One Atwood swivel jack & wheel with frame mount swivel.

Jacks provided by AgServ West.

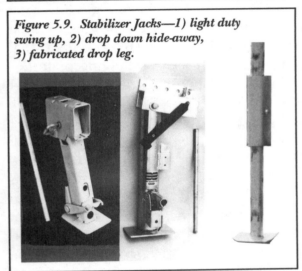

Figure 5.9. Stabilizer Jacks—1) light duty swing up, 2) drop down hide-away, 3) fabricated drop leg.

purposes. These jacks crank up and down like a bumper jack to raise and lower; they then flip up and store horizontally. Be sure to find a secure place to store the handle so it will be readily available when you need it. *Lighter duty stabilizer jacks* are fine for occasional light loads. I have found these lighter styles, although some are rated at 1000-lbs, unsuitable for anything over a few hundred pounds. Ratings probably come from loadings of pure compression with no side loads; and if that is what you have, the jack is O.K. Unfortunately most applications with trailers include uneven surfaces, resulting in side and offset loads. So take a close look at your situation and know the loads to be resisted. Many of these jacks were originally devised for specific situations and their use has expanded without the upgrading to include provisions for the new duties.

Accessories—Caster Wheels & Jack Mountings

Caster wheels are currently a subject of great concern to many—as they are quite popular but somewhat marginal in nature. A more durable wheel to replace those currently available would certainly be a welcome product. Caster wheels for jacks were largely designed for use on tongue jacks. The marginal caster wheels are rated at 1000-lbs. Where this rating comes from, I don't know. My experience finds those currently in existence to be fine as long as the trailer sits unloaded on the showroom floor and for a short time thereafter. If the trailer is loaded (which is the reason one wants the jack in the first place) with, say, a 300-lb tongue weight and is then pushed over anything except smooth concrete, the plastic bushing at the center of the wheel pops out and, of course, the wheel must be replaced. In addition, the thin plastic bushing used at the top to assist swivelling not only embrittles, but easily acquires dirt particles, squashes and breaks apart, rendering the swivel mechanism totally ineffective.

Many people I talk to are rather unhappy with this flimsy product and refuse to buy a new one—can you blame them? The few who do, discover the process merely repeats itself. My solution for reworking this wheel is to first cut the riveted axle off (not an easy task) and replace it with a heavy duty shoulder bolt of the proper diameter. A flat roller bearing (preferably sealed) can then be installed for the top swivelling. An easier way (slightly more expensive though) is to completely discard the existing wheel and save the top (for sliding onto the jack). Purchase an industrial quality steel caster with ball bearings and with a flat mounting plate (for bolting or welding into place). Weld this flat mounting plate of the caster wheel assembly to the bottom of the trailer caster wheel top and a durable heavy duty wheel results, as pictured in Figure 5.10.

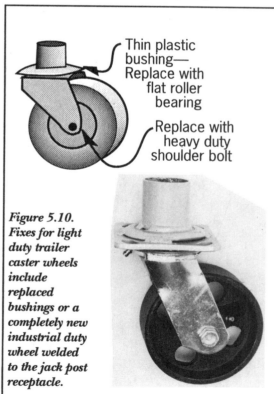

Thin plastic bushing—
Replace with flat roller bearing

Replace with heavy duty shoulder bolt

Figure 5.10. Fixes for light duty trailer caster wheels include replaced bushings or a completely new industrial duty wheel welded to the jack post receptacle.

Overall capacity ratings for jacks are apparently difficult to derive. Most are rated at 1000-lbs or 5000-lbs. What does that mean? It appears to mean that this sort of load can be withstood in a vertical direction. For some situations, especially where a jack foot is used, this is what is needed. If, however, the jack is used as a tongue jack with a caster wheel, other twisting loads also come into play, as shown in Figure 5.11. The sideways movements, and dimensions from ground to mount, result in an extra beating for **jack mounts**. Currently common ways of mounting a jack include angle mounts, U-bolt mounts, frame and tube swivel mounts, flat plates and the Pony jack mount—as shown in Figure 5.12. Simple angle mounts have been used successfully on small lightweight trailers but my experience finds them to be marginal when side loads from a big trailer with a heavy tongue weight are applied. U-bolt mounts depend on friction to hold the vertical position, have that "add-on" look and can leave "shin-catching" sharp protrusions unless the U-bolts are pointed inside (jack has to be mounted outside and off center). The patented Pony jack mount used

by IRD for several years was designed to overcome several of these problems and has proven to be effective. Contact *Techni-Visions* for current availability of these extra strong jack mounts.

Swivel jacks require a different approach. These mountings are offset to the jack's side. For jacks fitted with a foot, side loads are minimal. With a caster wheel though, they face some of the same problems as an angle mount. Heavier, larger mountings are definitely recommended, and are in most cases provided. In spite of a few drawbacks, properly and well thought out mounted jacks, used as designed, can be well worth their expense in assisting you to move or stabilize your trailer.

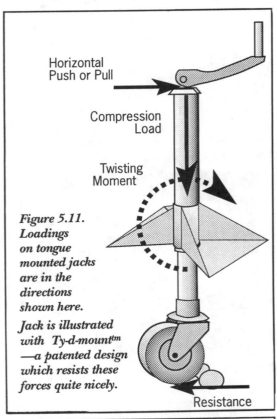

Figure 5.11. Loadings on tongue mounted jacks are in the directions shown here.

Jack is illustrated with Ty-d-mount^tm —a patented design which resists these forces quite nicely.

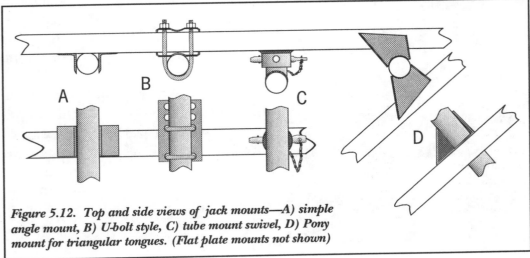

Figure 5.12. Top and side views of jack mounts—A) simple angle mount, B) U-bolt style, C) tube mount swivel, D) Pony mount for triangular tongues. (Flat plate mounts not shown)

Accessories—Winches

Winches are wonderful devices; they have the ability of moving something many times our size and weight with a mere twist of the handle or push of a button. For boat trailers they are a must—to get the boat out of the water and let it slide in slowly. Four wheelers use them to get out of ditches and other trouble. Just about any vehicle can be easily pulled onto a trailer bed. Other types of trailer cargo may also find their loading simplified with a winch.

Hand crank styles have been around for many years. These winches are usually sold separately from the cable, hook and clamps as shown in Figure 5.13. The logic here is that each person's requirement may change the length and diameter of cable needed. Capacities of these products range from 600-lbs to 3700-lbs. Be sure your winch cable has the capacity to match the winch's or make sure your load stays below the limit. Electric winches are fairly new to the scene. Operation is off the tow vehicle's 12-volt battery. Heavy duty wire, switches, installation instructions and even the cable and hook are usually all part of the package. Capacities range from 1500-lbs to 5000-lbs. Although *Superwinch*® is a well known brand, several other companies provide well made power winches.

Figure 5.13. Electric winch, hand winch, plus wire rope cable, hook & clamp.

To give you an idea of a winch's capacity, the chart in Figure 5.14 was prepared. The change in capacity of the load being hoisted with respect to the angle of incline is listed. This chart is applicable only to free rolling vehicles or boats riding over rollers. A damaged or wrecked auto will create a lot of resistance as it's metal scrapes and gouges its path. The ease of moving non-rolling cargoes depends on the coefficient of friction between the two surfaces. As you can see, from Figure 5.14, though, the ability of the winch to pull decreases as the angle increases.

WINCH CAPACITY based on % grade for Superwinch®

Grade >>> Angle >>>	20% 11°	30% 17°	50% 26°	70% 35°	100% 45°	Winch Capacity
Graphic Angle >>>	11° 2 10	17° 3 10	26° 5 10	35° 7 10	45° 10 10	as rated by Super-Winch
Capacity in lbs @ Grade Shown	3400 5100 8500 11900	2600 3900 6500 9150	1850 2800 4650 6500	1550 2300 3800 5350	1300 1950 3200 4500	1000 1500 3200 4500

Accessories—Tie Downs

Tying your load securely to hold it in place while the trailer is moving involves another form of pulling—down and opposite to other tyings. The importance of *tie downs* for this task cannot be underestimated. I never cease to be amazed at the number of stories I hear about people who fail to tie their loads. Expensive race cars roll off trailers behind motor homes, boats jump forward onto the tow vehicle in a mere emergency stop, unrestrained boxes of metal slide off of flat bed trailers. Pallet dollies roll out of unstaked sides of a flatbed. And there are numerous accidents caused by a change in the trailer's handling characteristics because of a shift in loading due to inadequate or non-existent tying. Along this line, one of the most bizarre things I have ever seen was a very small fellow riding in the back of a small pick-up truck holding in place an untied extra large and tall refrigerator. The truck was tooling down the freeway at night at 60 mph. I sure hope no emergency swerves were necessary because there is no way that giant refrigerator could have been held in place by that little person.

My guess is that most people have little idea how much force increases with velocity and what acceleration does to increase the effective weight of an item. In the early 70's, race cars generated as much as 1.7-g's in high speed cornering. Because of technological advancements, these cars now generate as much as 3-g's. G-loads of as little as .3-g's can be felt as a slight side tug in a slow corner. It makes cornering feel to a rider just a little uncomfortable . . . or exciting, whatever your emphasis. What does G-load mean? Downward weight from gravity would be referred to as 1-g. For instance, if an item weighs 100-lbs, its downward force is 100-lbs. And, if a corner is a 1-g corner, the sideways force will be 100-lbs. Imagine trying to hold something that weighs as much sideways as from underneath. In a 0.3-g corner, the sideways force of a 100-lb weight will be 30-lb. So all of a sudden, this thing standing by itself has what appears to be sideways weight. Seat belts and tie downs are a welcome restraint to those who understand these forces.

Tie downs shown in Figure 5.15 are only a sampling of those currently available from various manufacturers. Ratchet-to-tighten, over-center locks, slip locks and tension springs—each has its own specialty. The type of load you are hauling will have a lot to do with the one most appropriate for your application. Rope can also be used but it needs to be heavy duty nylon or sisal rope. Knotting and looping the rope properly so it won't work loose are also important. Do check the rating of the rope, and obtain the strongest one your budget will allow and your load needs. *Small load binders* shown in Figure 5.16 are another way to hold a load in place. They can be employed with chain or strap or hooked directly to the load. These tie downs take after their big brothers used to bind chain tightly over heavy loads such as steel on big trucks and are often called chain binders. For palletized loads and automobiles with existing cargo tie down loops these devices are quite handy. From 250-lbs to 1200-lbs capacity, these little jewels will handle a variety of loads.

Tying your load should be planned during trailer construction since

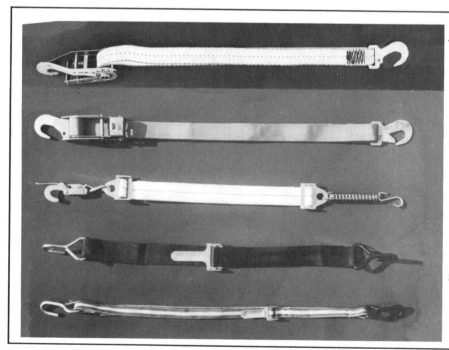

Figure 5.15. A variety of tie down straps. Each tie down has its special feature and works best in its own special way. Be sure to check these features out before you purchase. Shown here— ratchet, over-center lock, tension springs and two slip lock styles.

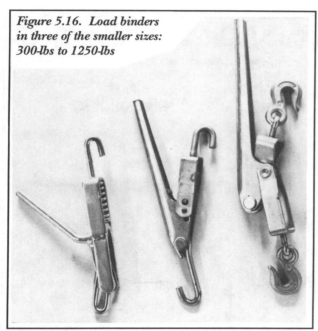

Figure 5.16. Load binders in three of the smaller sizes: 300-lbs to 1250-lbs

welding may be required to install pick-up points and use the tie downs properly. **Tie down loops** come in many styles some of which are shown in Figure 5.17. Here we have both weld-on and bolt-on styles. A popular style pulls up through the floor or through the wall and lays flat when the tie down is disconnected. On areas where tires roll or people walk, I have found **square bend U-bolts** to be a successful solution. Many cargoes need accurate placement of the loops to ensure the proper angle of tying. An advantage to these loops is that they can be positioned after the trailer is complete and painted. If done while the cargo is in place, the most appropriate placement will result. Note that square bend U-bolts have double the thread and nut area that a single bolt would have. With a large bearing plate under the nuts, a good capacity can generally be achieved.

An **eyebolt** and a **nut ringbolt** are also shown in Figure 5.17. Hardware store varieties have capacities equivalent to their grade of bolt which is generally at the lower end. I do not recommend this quality for use on a trailer. On the other hand, industrial quality items have much higher capacities (higher prices, too) and may be worth looking into. Note that these loops secure their loads with one thread and nut. Extra large and thick washers or plates should be used to spread pull through loads applied to the parent material. **Volume 2** discusses calculations to determine if the tie down hardware and its attachment is adequate for your application.

Attachment of eyebolts and nut ringbolts to a trailer's generally lighter material is sometimes difficult. An improvement is available with the **Ty-d-eye**^{tm}, whose patented design allows easy adaptation to a variety of trailer frames and cargoes. The longitudinal welds placed in two perpendicular directions provide substantial attachment strength. Welding surfaces can also be virtually in the same plane as the loop itself. A bolt-on style where the bolts are in shear in one or two perpendicular planes makes installation easier for completed trailers. Loads tied diagonally (Arrow A, Figure 5.17) gain maximum strength; loads tied perpendicular (Arrow B) tax this tie down to its maximum. Whatever your choice, an adequate quantity of tie downs using substantial attachment methods are essential.

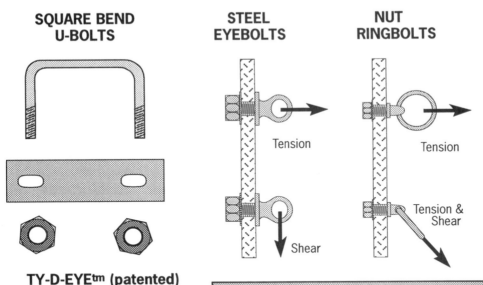

Figure 5.17. *Tie down loops take on a variety of configurations. Most are available premade in an assortment of capacities. Shown here are four styles commonly and most appropriately used for trailers. Data in table from* **McMaster Carr Catalog.**[10]

SQUARE BEND U-BOLTS

STEEL EYEBOLTS

NUT RINGBOLTS

Tension

Tension

Shear

Tension & Shear

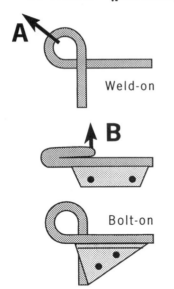

TY-D-EYE^{tm} (patented)

A

Weld-on

B

Bolt-on

WORKING LOAD LIMITS—Tension Only						
Shank Diam	Steel Eyebolts with Nuts		Steel Eyebolts Drop Forged		Nut Ringbolt	
	Ring ID	Load	Ring ID	Load	Ring ID	Load
1/4	0.5	500	.075	500	1.75	250
5/16	0.63	800	0.88	900	1.75	400
3/8	0.75	1200	1.00	1400	2.25	600
7/16			1.09	2000		
1/2	1.00	2200	1.19	2600	3.00	1100
9/16			1.28	3000		
5/8	1.25	3400	1.38	4000	2.75	1750.

STEEL EYEBOLTS & NUT RINGBOLTS — *Since this method depends on only one nut and one thread, knowing the capacity of each is a must. Capacities stated are for tension only; an angled load decreases capacity significantly. Large thick washers are highly advised.*

SQUARE BEND U-BOLT — *Recommended for sides and floors, where people walk or wheels roll. Two nuts and washer plate distribute load over large area.*

TY-D-EYE^{tm} — *These versatile tie down loops provide extra weld area for attachment to lighter trailer structures. Capacity is greatest in direction of Arrow A. Arrow B direction provides minimum strength. Contact* **Techni-Visions** *for more information regarding usage, strength and availability.*

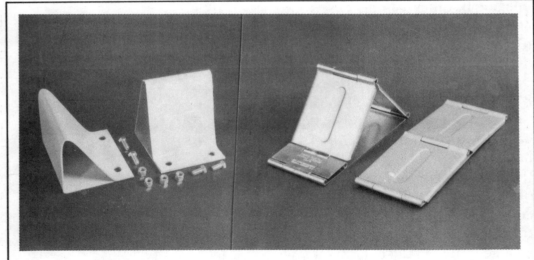

Figure 5.18. Wheel-stops (right) are bolted in place to ensure correct positioning. Wheel-blocks (left) do the same with an added feature—they flip up or lay flat as required.

If your cargo is an automobile, remember that vehicle tires are designed to roll. Unfortunately that is the last thing you want if the vehicle is atop a trailer. Contrary to some thinkers, leaving the car "with brakes on and in gear" alone will not keep that vehicle in place. Methods to prevent rolling, though, can be a real challenge. Besides the basic tie downs, which are a must, there are a few other helpful products. Figure 5.18 shows two such items—a **wheel-stop** and a **wheel-block**. Wheel-stops act as a sure stop at the exact forward position you want the vehicle to rest. Obtaining the optimum tongue weight, trailer balance and weight distribution is much easier with a pair of these stops. Bolting them in place rather than welding retains the flexibility should you change vehicles. Wheel-blocks also work great in the same duty but are more appropriately used to prevent rolling in the opposite direction—such as at the rear of the car. They lay flat as the car rolls over them while being loaded; then pop-up behind the car to hold it in place. Both of these products are great to use as stops, but act only as forward and backward restrictors. Tie downs are always required in addition for complete security.

Accessories—Anti-Theft

Now that your trailer is built, discouraging would-be thieves with a **trailer lock** is a smart policy. New products in this area seem to show up often but a few old standbys, shown in Figure 5.19, can help you in the meantime. The **coupler lock** discourages thefts by locking the portion of the coupler that accepts the hitch ball. Hearsay has it that some thieves have foiled this one by using a string to work it loose. This is hard to imagine but they can also use ropes and chains to attach the trailer to the tow vehicle for a short term tow. If they are really bent on stealing your trailer, they're going to find a way. But this little device will certainly slow 'em down and discourage most casual thieves. The **hitchlock** not only prevents accidental opening of the coupler mechanism while driving (taking the place of the coupler lock pin), it theft proofs your trailer while on or off the tow vehicle. This product is available in one size which seems to fit a wide range of couplers. The right sized padlock can also be used for this same duty.

Although the **chain wheel lock** has come and gone as manufacturing rights were sold from one company to the next, it has always been a good idea. It prevents the wheel turning which makes moving or towing the trailer virtually impossible. Any attempt to do so may flatten the tire and, most desirable of all, cause a lot of noise and commotion. The special lug nut with the loop for the chain requires tooling to cast, although fabricating your own lug nut with loop is a possibility. A caution here; wheels should be re-balanced with the loop installed. Better yet, use the loop only when the trailer is parked, making sure to replace and tighten

Figure 5.19. Various anti-theft devices—chain wheel lock, coupler lock, hitch lock.

the original nut for towing. Spoke wheels eliminate the need for this special nut as the chain can be looped through the spokes. Beyond the trailer itself, don't overlook the possibility of items within it or bolted to it being also susceptible to theft, including the wheels and tires. A simple wheel lock like those used for automobiles will usually fit the lugs on the trailer and may save you some undesirable errands. Covers or canvas canopies also discourage would-be thieves by keeping desirables out of sight.

C. FABRICATED ACCESSORIES

Specially fabricated accessories can add capability to any trailer, making it versatile and useful as initially intended. If you start with a basic trailer, I recommend bolting as many accessories as possible. The chances are very great you'll want to use your trailer for something you never imagined. I have also found light weight materials advantageous for accessories as a way to keep the weight of the trailer to a minimum. It is amazing how quickly accessory weight can cause the overall weight to creep up into an undesirable area.

Fabricated accessories include tool boxes in any number of configurations, stakesides, overhead carriers, tire racks, saddle racks, special platforms for weld bottles or other unusual cargoes, hose reels, spare tire carriers, doors and tailgates, dividers and bins, vents and windows, kick plates, partitions, gravel guards, bins or compartments. The list is endless, and depends on the specific cargoes you intend to carry, as we have already mentioned, as well as the ultimate function of your trailer. We will discuss a few of the more universal accessories here, but for obvious reasons cannot discuss them all.

Fabricated Accessories—Tool Boxes

Tool or accessory boxes mounted to the tongue or over the wheels and tires can provide useful and necessary storage. Any tool box generally

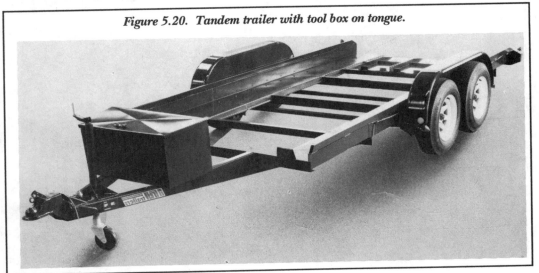

Figure 5.20. Tandem trailer with tool box on tongue.

ends up holding lots of paraphernalia, some of which can be very heavy. The approximate weight is important to know so the tool box can be placed appropriately. Too much weight improperly distributed can have dire effects on trailer balance and stability. It is also a good idea to gather all the items you intend to house in the tool box and measure the space they fill. This is a good time to weigh them also.

Figure 5.20 is a flatbed car trailer with a tool box attached to the tongue—a very popular place for tool boxes. You do need a longer tongue for this placement to ensure room for the rest of your cargo. Maybe this is a good way to ensure that a longer tongue gets built. The tool box and its weight should be included as part of your initial frame calculations, as discussed in **Volume 2**. Remember that a tool box and a long tongue can increase the load and thus the size requirements of the tongue material. A gusset and/or doubler may be necessary to help meet that requirement. Fender mounted tool boxes, Figure 5.21, are also a possibility. These have the advantage of being centered over the axle, so that a heavy load of tools won't significantly affect tongue weight. As with the tongue mounted box, knowing the weight of the box material as well as the proposed components of the contents can make it easier to design a lightweight adequate supporting structure up over the fenders.

As long as the tool box base is well supported, a light gauge steel— 16 or 18 gauge (and even 20 gauge in some instances)—is appropriate for most tool boxes and is recommended because of the significant amount of weight the box itself can add. Sheet steel is easy to bend on a box and pan brake if you have access to one. Stiffener ribs on large panels should be provided and spot welded in place. Spot welding (discussed in Chapter 6) works well for tool boxes because of its minimal heat generation. Stick or

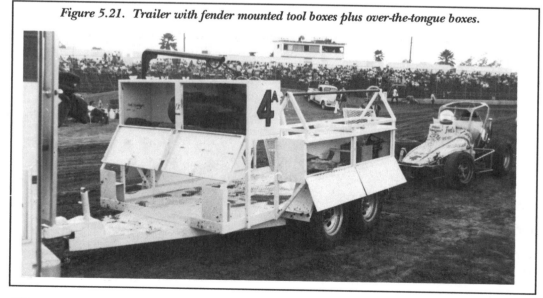

Figure 5.21. Trailer with fender mounted tool boxes plus over-the-tongue boxes.

MIG welding will in most cases warp large flat steel sheets and ruin your material and the work you spent bending. Wooden tool boxes are also a possibility but usually end up being heavier and decidedly less resistant to the weather. Aluminum tool boxes are definitely light weight but may be expensive. The minimum wall thickness one would want to consider is probably .050-inches, depending on the alloy and number of stiffeners used. In this case riveting is probably a better choice for joining, although properly welded aluminum can provide a handsome product.

Fabricated Accessories—Stakesides

Stakesides, which are removable, turn a flatbed trailer, Figure 5.22, into a box trailer which can then always be returned to a full flatbed. The rear can be left open, filled with an additional stake-rack, or a drop down steel tailgate for lightweight loads. No one has developed or marketed a universal stake-rack that will work with all heights, lengths and hole separations. Hence, lots of options are possible with stakesides.

Wooden slats of 1" x 6" or 1" x 4" dimension can be used. An inexpensive hardwood, such as Apitong, will be more resistant to warping. Special formed lightweight steel slats are also available at a few places. Posts can be made from 2" x 4" wood, 2" x 3" formed steel hat sections with special stamped bottoms or universally available rectangular tubing. Depending on the receptacle dimension and height, tubing of 3/4" x 1-1/2", 1" x 2" or 1-1/2" x 3-1/2" are sizes which can create a nice stake-rack.

Figure 5.22. Two styles of flatbed trailer with removeable stakesides.

Figure 5.23. Stake-racks shown are light duty rack (above) and standard heavy duty style—both with steel siding. Parts necessary for building the racks include side and corner latches, pockets (for large posts) and post ends for wooden posts. Rectangular tubing posts do not require special ends but should have pockets deep enough to prevent the rack bouncing out of its receptacle in transit.

Pockets need to be dimensioned to fit the post and securely mounted. Latches along the sides and at the corners hold the racks in place. Once built, the racks should be marked with large letters as to their respective positions so that replacement is easy. Stake sides are quite strong in spite of their removability. However, leaning heavy materials against them is probably a mistake and could cause some irreversible problems. Figure 5.23 shows two stake-rack styles with standard parts to give you a start on building your own. If stake-racks are desired, they should be part of the initial design so the structure can be planned to accept the pockets properly.

Fabricated Accessories—Racks & Carriers

With a trailer, **racks** and **carriers** of all types abound. They are smart solutions to cargo that may otherwise be rolling or sliding around. Something you want to keep with the trailer such as gas cans or a spare tire can be conveniently stored with a carrier. If you build a rack up and over anything and you plan to carry any appreciable weight, please be sure it is capable of withstanding the load to be carried. Lightweight items are much easier to carry on an overhead framework than heavier ones. The potential for swaying back and forth is greatly reduced and the load on the joints is not as severe. Whatever the load, calculations similar to the ones presented in **Volume 2** will help you determine the material size requirements. Special attention should be given to the design of the joints. An overhead rack is shown on the trailer in Figures 5.24.

Depending on the purpose of your trailer, accessories specifically for just about any job are available. Horse trailer manufacturers usually offer extra doors, saddle and other tack racks. The trailer can be made longer or taller for large horses or more gear. Boat trailers require few accessories

Figure 5.24. A trailer with stakesides and an overhead rack for long, lightweight items. Note the gusseting in the upper corners.

because extra gear can usually be carried in the boat. (But be careful to not overdo it.) Some accessories, such as heavy duty winches and jacks, can become part of the accessory package. Although these additional items increase the basic cost of your trailer, the trade-off in labor and headaches usually makes them well worth the additional investment. Utility trailers can be loaded with accessories for special purposes or be just a bare bones trailer. Equipment trailers need tool boxes and many kinds of special racks, carriers and often a special framework to start with. All this customizing costs money and no matter what its type each trailer is largely a special project. Too many people attempt to compare trailers with items produced in mass—they are not the same thing. Few trailers are produced in large enough mass to qualify as a mass produced item.

CHAPTER 6.

CONSTRUCTION ASPECTS

A. Purchasing Materials & Components

B. Laying Out a Floor Guide

C. Cutting

D. Welding

E. Painting (and Before)

F. Installing the Final Parts

G. Before You Hit the Road—the Final Check!

Acquiring the materials, components, and tools necessary to build your trailer may turn out to be a major task. But once you've got them, the constructing requires skill as a welder and a fabricator, as well as a good aptitude for mechanical things. Experience with spray painting and electrical work can also come in handy. The patience to plan your work carefully, buy the parts at the right place for the right price and coordinate all your building activities is an integral part of the process. If you are of the school that says welding skill alone will get you a trailer, you better read this chapter (and re-read the previous five). Welding may be a large portion of the work and it may indeed be one of the more important ones, but it is far from the only skill required.

A. PURCHASING MATERIALS AND COMPONENTS

Now that you're educated about trailer design, it's time to turn your plans into hardware. The amount of hardware to be purchased depends on where you have started your project—from scratch, so to speak, from published plans or from a kit. A weld-up or bolt-together kit usually leaves only a little for you to do. The procurement of parts has been basically accomplished, except for a few incidental accessories, wheels and tires, and perhaps some other personal touches. Once you have the kit, planning your work consists of finding a good place to set up your trailer, verifying the existence of all the parts, and deciding the easiest approach or method. The included instructions should provide step by step methods of constructing your trailer, with tips on each phase. If you have decided on a kit to save money, be forewarned that this may not happen. The actual cost of labor in a built trailer is about 15-30% of the total cost rather than 50-70% as some may think.

If you have a set of plans, purchasing is simplified since a listing of all parts along with the location of some specialized suppliers is probably included. If not, you're back to Square One. Finding suppliers for the many specialized trailer parts can become a sizable part of the project. In any event, purchasing all your parts *before beginning construction* has a decided advantage—and should be done if possible.

If you have developed your own design, the procurement of parts can be a downright major effort. It's not unheard of to visit three or four stores for each type of item just to educate yourself about the products available; and even with that you may come back empty-handed. The previous chapters provide much of the basic information about most parts used on a trailer—this information will definitely save some running; however, your design may also require special applications and need even further research. Even with basic products, multiple decisions are necessary. For instance, steel is a category containing subsections of angle, channel, tubing, sheet, bar—a different supplier will often be required for each. After finding the supplier, a whole series of options should be examined for each case. If shopping is enjoyable to you, this may be a delightful pastime. However, if you can't find the appropriate parts the experience can be very discouraging. Particularly frustrating is having to change a design or modify adjacent parts to fit what's on the market instead of what you originally planned and laid out. Please understand, this is part of the process and should be accepted.

To obtain information and specifications about products on the market, it is extremely useful to study a variety of catalogs. Obtaining these catalogs in advance of designing may help you avoid a few frustrations. Several companies listed in the Appendix offer catalogs for small fees. These catalogs contain a wide selection of specialized parts for trailers and turn out to be a convenient resource for some of those hard to obtain parts. If you send the amount stated to the addresses listed the companies will return a catalog to you. Copy the form in Figure 6.1 to save writing a letter. Parts offered by these companies are intended for manufacturers and if the quantity to be purchased is fewer than 3 or yours is a one time purchase, it will make more sense to ask for a retailer in your area, who is also very likely to have a stock of parts and other accessories of interest.

Whatever you do, don't treat purchasing lightly. Take the time to study what you need to study and know what you're buying. A hastily purchased, cheap, junk yard axle may seem a "good deal" up front, but cautions are in order. Retired auto axles were designed for about 2000-lbs or less these days (actually about 1/2 the auto's weight). Trailer axles typically have higher ratings. Under a trailer, these automotive straight axles can raise the trailer's center of gravity unacceptably. Widthwise, they are short, permitting a bed width of 3 or 4-feet, unless lengthened. Attempts to lengthen them are always difficult at best and risky, to boot. Mounting of the specially designed auto spring hangers can turn into an arduous task. But retired auto axles aren't the only ones where problems lurk. Even a set of slightly used mobile home axles can put you on the wrong design path, as I've seen happen.

Before you begin your store-by-store investigation, a thorough organization of all the needed parts into discrete categories will ease your travels. Components available at the same store should be placed on the same list. The lengths of steel should be figured and adjusted to be cut from the fewest lengths (20', 30' or 40') with the least waste possible. Sheet metal parts should be figured and ordered at a sheet metal house where shearing and bending to your specifications can also be performed.

Trailer parts—axle, hubs, springs, spring hardware, coupler and fenders—are most apt to be found at a trailer manufacturer, trailer supply,

Figure 6.1. A standard form to use in requesting catalogs from various suppliers: (Just cover up this line and copy the page for an easy to use format.)

To:

_____

_____

_____

_____

_____

Dear Supplier,

Please send a copy of your catalog to the address indicated below.
I have enclosed $_____ to cover the cost of the catalog plus shipping & handling.

Name_____

Address_____

City_____State_____Zip_____

Please indicate the name of the nearest dealer or distributor to me so I can purchase the necessary parts for my trailer construction project.

Thank you,

_____
name

or one of the companies whose catalog is listed in the Appendix. Mobile home supply stores handle sewers, water lines, stoves and refrigerators, but because of the complexity, seldom handle running gear and accessories. Local trailer manufacturers will carry axles which are specially suited to their line of trailers and may not necessarily fit your requirements. However, what you need usually can be ordered. In searching for parts, bear in mind that your trailer will be with you for years and years. It is sometimes better to wait 30, 60, 90 days to get the right parts, than to purchase something in a hurry that is marginal in its application.

A search of the **Yellow Pages** may give you the quickest answers, and of course a phone call may save a futile trip and wasted gas. The **Yellow Page** headings listing businesses most apt to carry products you will need for your trailer are:

Trailers—Auto, Utility	*Hardware*
Trailers—Boat	*Lighting*
Trailers—Truck	*Steel—Sheet Metal*
Trailers—Parts & Accessories	*Steel—Rolled Products*
Welding—Equipment	*Steel—Tubing*

Specialty magazines and publications from local special interest clubs frequently carry display or classified ads to guide you to neighborhood sources of supply. And your local newspaper may even sport an appropriate ad or two.

Once you have investigated the parts and made your selection, purchasing is easy. As long as you have the money, just go to the stores where you've selected the parts or materials and purchase them. If the parts come from quite a distance, be sure to check the weight and shipping charges. Trailer parts are made of steel and when added up, quickly become quite heavy. Some folks like to shop price . . . that's one way. When safety is a consideration, design and materials must also be considered. And don't forget service: Which company has the most knowledgeable person to help you out if you get into trouble? Best price companies seldom have knowledgeable sales people, and very often don't stand behind their products. Ponder carefully and check out the situation before you buy.

B. LAYING OUT A FLOOR GUIDE

With all your materials and parts in hand, your framework can actually start to take shape. I have found that starting with a chalked-in layout on the floor not only speeds assembly but can improve accuracy. Before cutting and positioning your parts, use the chalk to mark a few basic

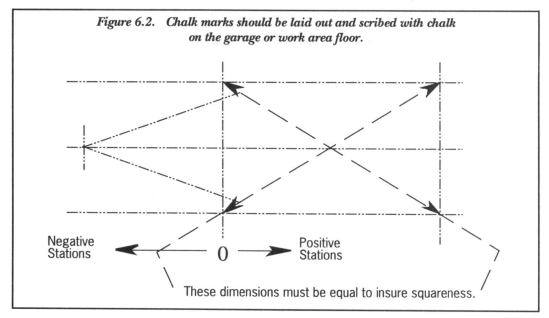

Figure 6.2. *Chalk marks should be laid out and scribed with chalk on the garage or work area floor.*

Negative Stations ← — — 0 → Positive Stations

These dimensions must be equal to insure squareness.

layout lines where construction is to take place. This is the time to make sure everything is perfectly square. The centerline should first be marked on the floor with a long straight edge; then measure out to the position of each outside frame member. Draw two more lengthwise lines parallel to the centerline an equal distance away. Draw a perpendicular line through all three at the point you wish to designate as the front cross-brace. This is station 0. Forward from there the numbers are counted as negative. Rearward they are positive. This numbering system will give you a definitive check on placement of lines as you proceed. This system is, of course, an arbitrary device. Alternatively, you might prefer to reference all dimensions to the coupler or to the rear of the trailer. The front cross-member tends to be the least confusing, however, particularly if you later decide to change the length of either the bed or the tongue.

After you mark the most rearward point as the end of your trailer, use a perpendicular line from the centerline to delineate the outer rear corners. Diagonal measurements from corner to corner can now be used to check the actual "squareness" of the rectangle you've just drawn. Make necessary adjustments at the corners and extend these two perpendicular lines to create a full rectangle. Figure 6.2 shows the lines of most importance to include. I have found this full scale visual guide indispensible as a check for positioning the main structural members of the trailer. Clamping these parts together, applying tack welds and welding things up from there is an easy step. Marking approximate positions for axle, coupler and cross bracing are also a help. Remember, this layout is only a guide. Measuring for exactness before welding is still a necessary step. Certain types of material lend themselves more readily to this approach. Trailer frames made with channel, angle and tubing can be laid out in this fashion. A trailer made of formed sheet metal or formed tubing does not fit this procedure as conveniently, since these parts must be designed and laid out separately before fitting everything together. Once the parts are formed, though, this type of layout can then be used.

C. CUTTING

Before laying the pieces down on your floor layout, they must be cut. To achieve this, one has a wide selection of options. Metal cuts are very different from wood cuts. Wood is much softer and succumbs very easily to a sharp blade. Metal requires a different approach. It must be "filed" at low temperatures, "melted" with high temperatures, machined away or just plain "whacked off" or split with a lot of power. Special saws and shears are made for separating metal and one should take heed of the special tools if cutting is a requirement. Some tools used for this purpose are shown in Figures 6.3 to 6.8 and listed here:

1) an abrasive circular saw *(A)*,
2) a hot cut steel blade *(B)*,
3) a cold cut steel blade
    with coolant *(C)*,
4) a power hack saw *(D)*,
5) a band saw *(E)*,

6) an oxyacetylene torch (Figure 6.5),
7) a plasma cutter (a new device,
        shown in Figure 6.6),
8) a power shear (Figure 6.7),
9) an iron worker (Figure 6.7),
10) a variety of hand tools (Fig 6.8).

Each tool, of course, has its own unique advantage. The shape of the pieces to be cut, how clean the edges need to be, the holding method and speed desired will influence your choice.

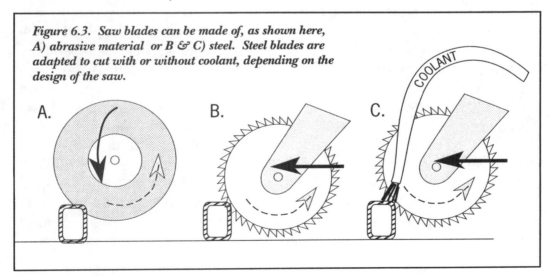

Figure 6.3. Saw blades can be made of, as shown here, A) abrasive material or B & C) steel. Steel blades are adapted to cut with or without coolant, depending on the design of the saw.

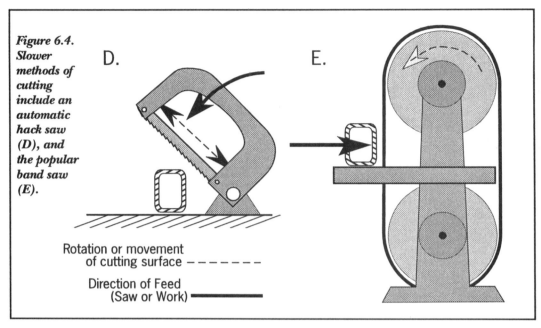

Figure 6.4. Slower methods of cutting include an automatic hack saw (D), and the popular band saw (E).

Rotation or movement of cutting surface – – – – – – –

Direction of Feed (Saw or Work) ▬▬▬▬▬

The quickest method of cutting lengths of steel such as angle or tubing is one of the first three items. All three *circular saws* are sometimes called *"cut-off saws"*. The first listed *abrasive saw* leaves a rather large sharp burr which can be ground, filed or trimmed . . . or melted when the end is welded to an adjoining piece. Be careful handling this metal, as the burr has no mercy and cuts like a razor. Be sure no sharp edges are left facing inside along paths used for electrical wire because their coatings are easily cut. *Hot cut steel blade saws* also leave burrs but whittle away solid chunks of steel very quickly. If speed is your goal, this is an excellent choice. *Cold cut steel blade saws* also cut quickly, require lots of coolant have a slower turning blade, are considerably more expensive but have one advantage over all the others—no burr remains. Another caution in using these saws—**DO NOT WEAR GLOVES** while cutting. Safety people say, and I tend to agree, it is too easy to catch the unfelt edge of the glove in the spinning blade. Once caught, the glove is easily pulled into the machinery along with what's inside—your hand!! So now since the saw creates sharp burrs, and gloves are not recommended, you must be extra cautious and alert while using any saws. Other types of rotating machinery also fall into this category of caution—grinders (pedestal mount or disc type) and drills.

The *band saw* and *hack saw* are also suitable for cutting steel. These saws make very clean cuts, leave very little burr but are somewhat slow. If you have a lot to cut, horizontal band saws and hack saws can be set up to cut a specified length automatically. Then you can set it and just leave it to do its work. If you have any one of these saws, you have more than most home workshops and more than many weld or trailer manufacturing shops.

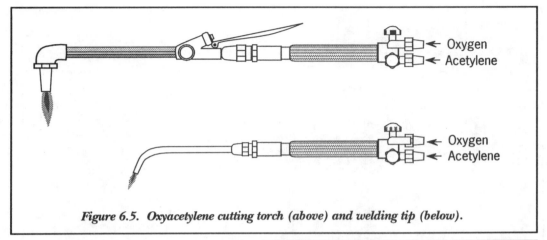

Figure 6.5. Oxyacetylene cutting torch (above) and welding tip (below).

Odd shaped cuts can be accomplished with an angle guide on many of the saws just discussed or with an **oxygen-acetylene torch**. Many small welding shops use the torch method of cutting exclusively because set up time is nil. The big disadvantage is the resulting ragged edges which require heavy grinding to obtain a secure fit and clean weld surface. The resulting edges are, however, not sharp. Often, a smoother cut is possible with a flame cutter attachment. A pattern is used to guide the cutting tip smoothly around the pattern of a predetermined outline. Although a

Figure 6.6. The plasma cutter is a recent development which does a superior job of cutting.

burr exists, a small amount of grinding cleans it up easily and if the pattern is followed, a smooth edge results. **Plasma cutters**, Figure 6.6, are even better at leaving little or no burr and create a nice smooth cut.

Power shears, Figure 6.7, cut sheet metal better than almost anything I know of. Shears are available in sizes ranging from one foot to fifteen feet. The thicker the material to be cut, the more massive the required machine. Unfortunately the expense of these machines dictates a heavy usage to justify the purchase of one. Alternatively, some sheet metal job shops can shear your material or the steel supplier can provide the material cut to size.

Iron workers, also Figure 6.7, are machines with lots of power used to cut a multitude of materials. Dies and cutting blades are permanently positioned around the machine to cut angle and round, flat or square bar.

Figure 6.7. Power shears, a short one shown here, are useful tools if you plan much work with sheet metal. Iron workers come in a variety of shapes and sizes —a Mubea HIW 750 is shown below.

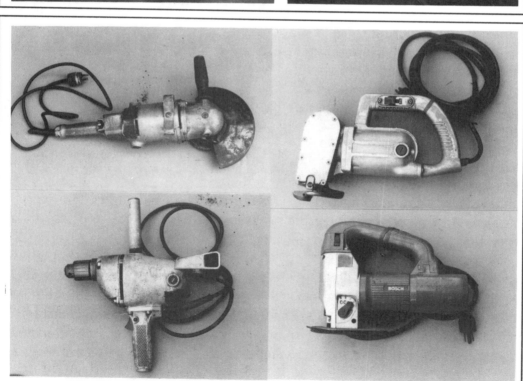

Figure 6.8. Heavy duty hand tools are especially helpful for working with metals. Shown here: 1) disc grinder/sander, 2) 1/2" drill motor, 3) power hand shear, 44) heavy duty jig saw.

These machines usually also have a 90° notcher and a 1-inch slot notcher plus a hole punch with a variety of sizes. New machines are quite expensive but can quickly pay for themselves by reducing the amount of setup time for new tasks. Iron workers seldom leave burrs but are limited to a maximum thickness of material usually 1/4" or 3/16". They also don't work too well with tubing; and channel seldom fits the dies.

A variety of **hand tools**—jig saw, hand shear, disc grinder, 1/2" drill motor, for example—can be scrounged up for special purpose cutting. For steel cutting, though, these tools need to be extra heavy duty, more so than the wood cutting variety. Some of these tools are shown in Figure 6.6.

D. WELDING

Welding, although not the only skill required for building a trailer, still ranks as the most important. As discussed in greater detail in **Volume 2**, properly executed and designed, a weld can produce a bond between materials which is at least as strong as the parent material itself. To properly place that weld, many methods of welding are available. Names you have probably heard in discussions about welding methods probably include arc, MIG or wire feed, gas, heliarc, spot or fusion welding. Gas, arc and wire feed welding are easily applied to trailer construction and other customized products. Heliarc machinery produces welds of superior quality; however, the technique is expensive and slow by comparison to other forms of welding. Spot and fusion welding are used with thin metal sheets and extensively in mass production with highly standardized parts.

Arc welding is the modern and technically superior process for joining parts where high loads and stress are encountered such as with a trailer. Arc welding is performed electrically, Figure 6.9, when a ground clamp, (usually attached to the trailer) and a "hot wire" (usually the weld rod held by the rod holder) contacts the trailer surface. The contact (or electrode end) is with a stick of metal already coated with flux. The metal sticks or welding rod, are commonly available in diameters of 1/16" to 3/8". The arc that is struck creates so much heat that the nearby metal as well as the rod is melted. The terms "short arc" and "stick welding" are common names for this procedure. When the weld has cooled, the slag left from the flux should be chipped away and the weld area brushed. Never change the rod while sitting or standing on your weldment or the trailer, especially with the ground clamp attached. However, I have found that sitting or standing on the trailer during the welding process won't shock you unless you grab (**NOT RECOMMENDED**) the welding rod with a bare hand or stand in water. As with any modern industrial procedure, knowledge and safety is highly advised.

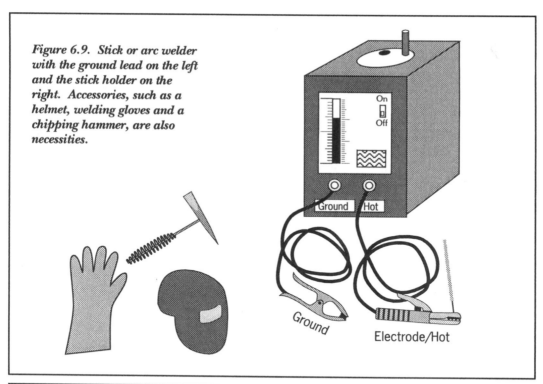

Figure 6.9. Stick or arc welder with the ground lead on the left and the stick holder on the right. Accessories, such as a helmet, welding gloves and a chipping hammer, are also necessities.

On
Off

Ground Hot

Ground

Electrode/Hot

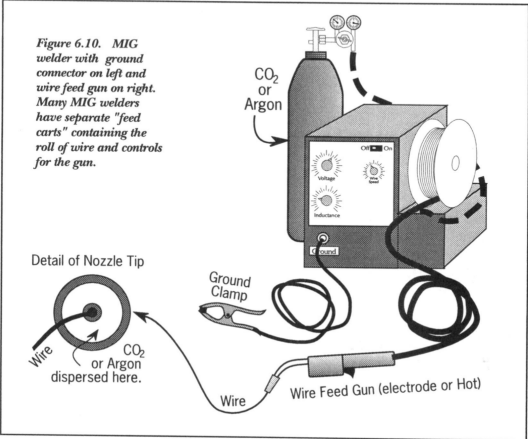

Figure 6.10. MIG welder with ground connector on left and wire feed gun on right. Many MIG welders have separate "feed carts" containing the roll of wire and controls for the gun.

CO_2 or Argon

Off On

Voltage

Wire Speed

Inductance

Ground

Detail of Nozzle Tip

Wire

CO_2 or Argon dispersed here.

Ground Clamp

Wire

Wire Feed Gun (electrode or Hot)

Wire feed or **MIG** welding, shown in Figure 6.10, uses the same principle as arc welding but is done with a fine wire of diameters ranging from .025-in to .050-in. This welding is often termed MIG for "Metal Inert Gas." Instead of a stick electrode, this modern system uses a "gun" attached by a hose to a wire reel. The wire is fed through the hose and gun making contact with the grounded metal. Again the extensive heat from the electric arc melts the surrounding metal and wire producing a molten puddle which bonds when cooled. The hose from the gun is also attached to a bottle of inert gas such as Argon or CO_2. This gas flows through the tube to the gun where it is dispersed in a donut shape surrounding the melting wire. The gas shields the molten material from oxygen and nitrogen thereby preventing oxidation and a useless weld full of little tiny holes. This gas replaces the solid flux used in arc welding.

Gas welding uses the combustion of oxygen and acetylene gases to generate flame and heat. Figure 6.11 illustrates the equipment. The gas from an oxygen tank and a separate acetylene tank are "piped" to a nozzle where the two are mixed, creating a very hot flame. The flame has to be very carefully mixed and monitored. Welding rods of various materials dipped in "flux" for a smooth flow are used to fill the hole and create the bond between the two pieces of steel . . . or aluminum. The flux is used to

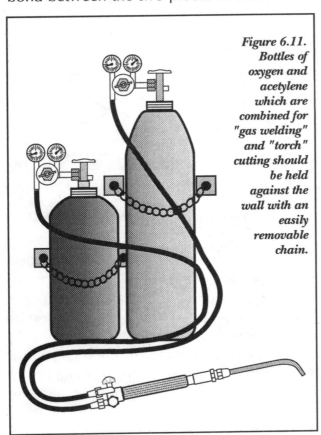

Figure 6.11. Bottles of oxygen and acetylene which are combined for "gas welding" and "torch" cutting should be held against the wall with an easily removable chain.

cleanse the part and purge the atmosphere around the weld making the bond very secure. Gas welding is not the best for "gluing" a trailer together. Although it's possible to produce an excellent result, the possibility of introducing too much carbon into the weld because of an incorrect flame mixture is very great. This disturbs the molecular structure of the material causing brittleness in the weld, adding to that in the surrounding material. But with acquired skill and certain kinds of rod, you can produce gas welds of acceptable strength. Skilled operators often use this type of weld on race car frames.

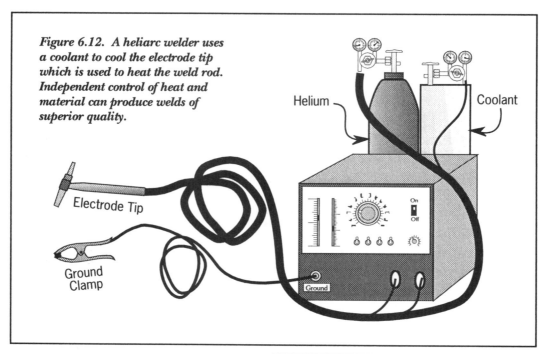

Figure 6.12. A heliarc welder uses a coolant to cool the electrode tip which is used to heat the weld rod. Independent control of heat and material can produce welds of superior quality.

Helium

Coolant

Electrode Tip

Ground Clamp

Ground

Gas welding equipment is also used for flame cutting; and in trailer building, this may well be the more extensive use. The tip and tool for cutting is very different from that used for welding, as was shown earlier in Figure 6.5. The flame also looks different as a cutting flame is much larger and more intense.

Heliarc welding is to many the ultimate. It is similar to the MIG process except that a permanent tungsten electrode replaces the wire feed gun. The welding rod

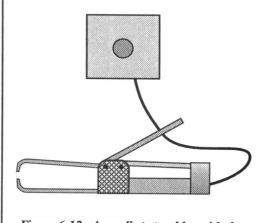

Figure 6.13. A small spot welder with the extension arms for reaching around to both sides of the pieces.

is fed separately from the side as in gas welding, providing a skilled operator independent control of heat and weld metal buildup. The machine to provide power, Figure 6.12, is expensive, and the procedure is relatively slow, resulting in an expensive process for big jobs. The results are superb though and premium application items top the list of uses. Thin wall race car frames and aircraft structures are popular examples. Here a minimum of heat with maximum penetration is important for integrity of these structures. This method can be used on a trailer if you take the time and can justify the expense.

Of the methods discussed above, I have found the most practical for welding a trailer is wire feed or arc welding. Both of these methods are fast and give welds of excellent quality . . . assuming, as with anything, the operator is skilled and knows what he's doing.

The strength of a weld is highly variable. Such seemingly minor things as the angle of the rod, distance of the rod from the metal, heat setting on the machine and smoothness of bead placement, can cause a weld to lack penetration and thus not be the binder it was designed to be. Weld placement in relation to the surrounding material or direction of loading can also have a decided effect on the overall capacity of the structure. This is discussed in **Volume 2**, and should be reviewed to enhance your understanding or if you have questions.

For accurate alignment of the finished weldment, I have found procedure and order of welding to be especially important. Penetration welds should be laid **AFTER** tack welds are used to position the parts. A tack weld is a tiny weld, just barely enough to keep the parts from moving. Very little heat is generated and parts generally do not move. The order and method of tacking and welding is also important as it can warp the frame or keep it straight. The whole frame should be tacked securely before it is welded and welding should then be done in a succession of opposite corners. Weld heat can be made to work for you and has to be an important consideration in the construction of your trailer. To ensure squareness, the parts should be correctly positioned, measured accurately, clamped in place, and then tack welded. Recheck all the vital dimensions and then final weld opposite corners, watching carefully that the frame does not shift or warp from the heat. A note of interest is that mobile home manufacturers use this warping from welds to their advantage. A weld of a specific length along the top of the frame will curl a long frame member up. Using a specific length of weld compensates for the direction the frame bends when the mobile home is built and placed on top.

E. PAINTING (AND BEFORE)

Painting will bring your trailer to its last phase of construction and you to a real sense of completion. After painting, your trailer will be much easier to clean and use. Most of all, paint will protect it from rust. Before you start the painting process, though, be sure you have finished welding and have drilled all the necessary holes. Recheck your lights and wiring system to be sure you have included all holes for tail lights, license lights and clearance lights. Any other holes for accessories are also easier to drill now. Before painting be sure your electrical system has been given a trial run; not connected but temporarily laid out so that places for all lights and wire are checked—brackets welded in place, all holes drilled or torched. Wire can even be test run through the expected pathways to check length and wire guide placement. Don't connect the wires now and be sure to remove them for painting.

Besides checking out all the holes, find a good safe way to get the trailer up off the ground so you can paint the underside. After all, this is the area that takes the most beating—rock, dirt, road grime and everything else gets kicked up from the tow vehicle, the trailer tires and the wind. This is the easiest area to miss because it's the hardest to paint and not easily visible. I have found jack stands (at least four, preferably six), acceptable to support the trailer. The jack stands need to be extra heavy duty and positioned so you won't kick them over. A couple of heavy duty tables or saw horses can also be used. Better yet a special designed roll-around dolly is an even better solution. Remember, you need to crawl under the trailer to spray it and a good solid support is cheap insurance. Once the trailer is up in the air, shake it slightly to be sure it is, in fact, solidly supported. (Be prepared to jump out of the way if it isn't.) I have also found a roll-around dolly with 4 to 6-inch steel casters especially useful for moving the trailer around. Plans for such a dolly may soon be available from *Techni-Visions*. The safety imparted with this dolly may make it well worth your while to spend the time making one rather than trusting jack stands . . . especially if you intend to build more than one trailer. Easy rolling dollies with heavy duty casters also find a way of coming in handy for other projects.

Preparation for painting is at least as or more important than the painting itself. With wood or walls at home we all know a clean surface helps the paint stick better. This is also true of steel. But steel is still very different from wood and in some ways much more difficult to clean. The painting and application process varies, too, requiring paint of a quality, material and consistency appropriate for metal applications.

Metal is different because metal surfaces are different. **Hot rolled steel** is typically covered with a thin scale from the heat developed when the material was originally rolled into shape. Angle and channel shapes have a rough surface of this scale, while sheet steel has the same scale but it is smoother. **Cold rolling** removes the scale but this process requires plenty of oil which remains on the surface. **Pickled and oiled** steel (often referred to as P&O) is first subjected to treatment to remove the scale, then it is specially oiled to preserve the bare surface from rust. It is not cold rolled (only treated chemically) and hence does not gain the added strength associated with the cold working. **Paint-lok** steel is a form of non shiny, flat-look galvanizing often used on sheet steel to protect it and improve paint adherence. Very little cleaning and preparation is required on this surface. It's wonderful material to work with because it is so clean.

However, the galvanizing can emit a toxic gas when welded so special precautions are required. When paint is applied, though, the surface absorbs the paint as if it were wood, discouraging runs and creating a smooth finish.

Cleaning these steel surfaces requires different approaches. The grease on P&O, cold rolled and tubing can be easily removed with a rag and solvent leaving a bright shiny clean surface which is easy to paint with a primer. The solvent used to thin acrylic enamel or industrial paint is called synthetic reducer, and works quite well to clean the grease off. Be sure to have plenty of rags as they will get dirty quickly. And by all means wear rubber gloves and **work in a well ventilated area as the fumes are toxic and flammable.** You may even want to wear a mask for protection from such fumes. Be sure to follow any instructions on the label and **DON'T SMOKE** while you're working with these solvents. When you have used the thinner to remove as much as possible, use an even cleaner rag soaked with solvent to wipe everything again. Then use a clean dry rag until you can feel no grease or particles on the metal with your bare hand. When you have finished, solvent-soaked rags should go into a metal container or a place where they can air dry thoroughly. Please don't stash them in a dark corner within a cardboard box, as spontaneous combustion on a hot day is a realizable threat.

Hot rolled steel—channel, angle and sheet—is not so easy. The scale is really stuck on and is very difficult to remove. It can be removed by sandblasting or with a light muriatic acid bath. When sandblasting, make sure the trailer hubs are protected. A heavy duty plastic bag taped around the hubs usually keeps grains of sand out. To avoid any problems, replace bearing grease after checking the bearings very closely and cleaning them carefully with solvent.

The muriatic acid bath can be mixed carefully from "swimming pool acid." **Be sure to wear gloves, goggles and long sleeve shirts, as the acid can burn your skin and cause permanent damage to your eyes. Wear a mask also because the fumes are toxic.** Be sure to fill the bucket with water **BEFORE** adding the acid. And follow directions for safe use provided on the container. Acid bathing is not too popular because of its obvious risks and dangers. However, if carefully and safely done, it will etch the layer of scale and leave a microscopically rough surface to which paint easily adheres. Please be sure to work with someone who knows something about these chemicals before attempting to do this on your own.

Immediately after acid bathing, or bringing the trailer home from sandblasting, the trailer should be wiped with a thinner soaked rag (usually synthetic reducer) and then a dry rag. To avoid rust, painting should commence immediately. As we all know "rust never sleeps", and is especially aggressive with bare, clean steel in humid or dampish weather.

Paints applied to metal surfaces should be sprayed on. Brush marks on wood surfaces blend with the wood grain or are soaked up and are accepted as normal. Paint sits on top of metal surfaces and streaks are very visible thus appearing as a defect. To avoid this, spraying is recommended. The myriad of corners found on trailers also make spraying much more effective.

As we mentioned earlier, the paint you use must be specially formulated for metals. First a primer coat of some kind—red oxide, zinc chromate or a combination primer—will adhere better to the steel, provide better rust resistance and create an excellent surface for your finish coat of paint. Over any of these primers, you may use lacquer, acrylic enamel, industrial enamel or rust inhibitive paint. Your choice may be dictated by the colors available in each type of paint. The location and convenience of a supplier may also be a deciding factor. Lacquer must be rubbed out to gain its full luster and may cause you a lot more work than you care to spend on a trailer, especially with the abundance of little corners and the entire underside. Any of the other paints are basically enamels and don't require rubbing. If you use an enamel, the trailer should be left to dry in the sun for a few days before its first use. Some paints take longer than others to dry. And the ambient air temperature significantly affects the total drying time. On a hot summer day, 24 hours may be enough; while wintertime may require three or four days. If the temperatures are really low, a catalyst can be added to speed the process. Refer to the paint manufacturer for advice regarding the type of catalyst and the amount.

A few tips in applying the paint: Enamels should be sprayed in two layers for each coat. First apply a light "tack coat" which just barely covers about 1/2 to 3/4 of the surface. You should be able to see a small amount of primer through the misty covering. Let this dry about 30 minutes and apply the finish coat; this time thick enough to get a good shine. The tack coat helps to keep the finish coat in place, reducing the potential for runs. If a run does occur, wipe and smooth the extra paint with a shop towel (a bit messy, but effective). Thin plastic or rubber gloves will protect your skin. When the surface is dry, a quick re-spray will mask all your marks. Twenty-four hours later a second coat sprayed in the same manner can deepen the shine and improve the protecting ability of the paint.

Remember that a trailer has twice the surface area of an automobile because both sides of the metal (top and bottom) have to be painted. When buying paint, the quantity required for a single axle flatbed trailer is usually less than a gallon. Most tandems require up to two gallons, and large box tandems may take three gallons. Covered trailers will need even more, since the insides and outsides of the cover must be done, as well as the top and bottom of the bed. Wood surfaces also soak up more.

F. INSTALLING THE FINAL PARTS

When the paint on your trailer has dried, you are ready to install the electrical system and bolt on any accessories you may have. Chapter 4 is full of details and specifications for connectors, wiring diagrams and lighting. Referring back to that chapter will refresh your memory about specific parts.

Hopefully all holes for lights were drilled and brackets for installation welded in place during the final stages of construction . . . certainly sometime **BEFORE** painting took place. Assuming everything is in order, lights can now be bolted into place. Light attachments must be tight because most lights are grounded through this connection as we discussed earlier. Effective grounding may require roughing up the painted surface to get a good connection. Once in place, pigtail wires protruding from the light must be connected to the proper hot wire to ensure a consistent system. Wiring diagrams shown in Chapter 4 illustrate several options open in this area. Most lights have only one wire to be connected but as you may remember tail lights are of the two filament variety and have two wires. The brighter filament should be connected to the turn signal and brake wire circuit since it is lit a shorter time and is more effective when slightly brighter. If a foreign car is used, a third light and wire will be needed since the brake lights and turn signals do not use the same filament. Alternatively, a *light adapter* accessory can be installed in the tow vehicle and the two filament wire system can be connected normally.

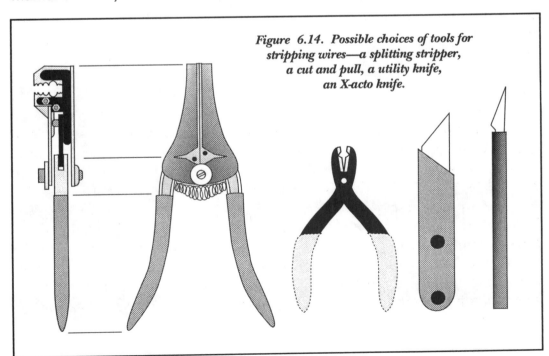

Figure 6.14. Possible choices of tools for stripping wires—a splitting stripper, a cut and pull, a utility knife, an X-acto knife.

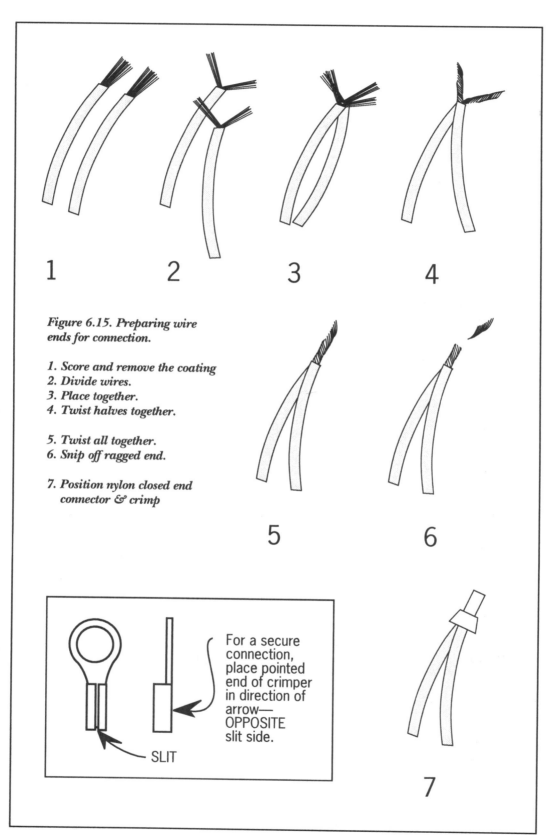

Figure 6.15. Preparing wire
ends for connection.

1. Score and remove the coating
2. Divide wires.
3. Place together.
4. Twist halves together.

5. Twist all together.
6. Snip off ragged end.

7. Position nylon closed end
   connector & crimp

For a secure
connection,
place pointed
end of crimper
in direction of
arrow—
OPPOSITE
slit side.

SLIT

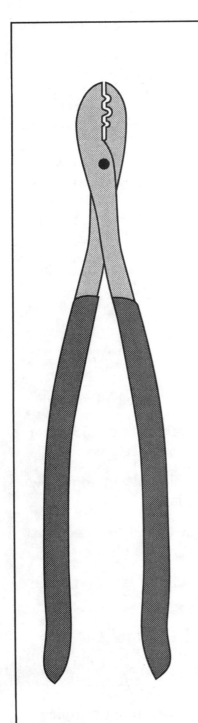

Figure 6.16. A heavy duty crimper for nylon closed end connectors makes the job of crimping much easier.

Connectors are available in many styles to tie wires together and were discussed in Chapter 4. Ground rings and nylon closed end connectors need wires with stripped ends. Use one of the wire stripping tools shown in Figure 6.14 to strip the ends (circumferentially) about a 1/2-inch back. Be especially careful of the sharp edges if the *X-acto* or utility knives are your choice, because they cut like butter. After splitting and double twisting the stranded wires as shown in Figure 6.15, snip the end and slide on a nylon closed end connector. Use a wire crimping tool, as shown in Figure 6.16 to assure a solid connection. Without a crimper or strippers, the *Scotch-lok™* T-splicing style connectors can be assembled with only a pliers and no stripping. Labor-wise these are easier but a bit bulky and more expensive.

Ground connectors must be installed at the electric brakes and at the main pigtail. Strip the wire ends as before, slide the ground ring on and crimp. If the pointed side of the crimper is opposite the slit, as shown in Figure 6.15, a more reliable connection will result. Be sure to add a 3 to 6-inch piece of wire to the ground wire out of the electric brakes to allow for suspension travel.

Once you think all the lights and wires are properly connected, set up a test to check out the light systems one by one—clearance, right turn, left turn, brakes, etc. Refer to the method described in Chapter 4.

It is time now to install the wheels and tires, tool boxes, caster wheel, panels, racks and other bolt-on accessories. After this is done and you have lowered the trailer onto its wheels and tires, **TIGHTEN ALL THE LUG NUTS**. Now take a break and refresh your mind. When you come back to your trailer, a fresh, unprejudiced start will prepare you for the final check.

G. BEFORE YOU HIT THE ROAD—THE FINAL CHECK!

Assuming you've checked things out as you went along, there may not be too much to check now. However, this is probably your last chance before the maiden voyage, so ascertaining that everything is correct and as it should be is a must. Major items that should be checked are listed below:

1) LUG NUTS TIGHT? Wheels and tires are usually installed while the trailer is off the ground. When the trailer is lowered to the ground, they must be re-tightened with a hand operated lug wrench. The consequences of missing this step are dire indeed. So, do this first!

2) Cotter pin properly installed at end of spindle? Pop off each dust cap just to be sure.

3) Nuts on spring U-bolts tight?

4) Nuts on hanger bolts fully onto thread? Nuts are new, not reused.

5) Coupler latch installed securely? Does it cradle the ball properly?

6) Accessories—tool boxes, jacks, panels, racks, bins and other bolt-ons—installed per instructions from manufacturer?

7) Hubs greased with plenty of grease? Spindle nuts appropriately tight? Cotter pin in place? Dust cap in place?

8) Recheck all welds—although it's a little late to find a missed one, it is better to repair it now than down the road a piece.

9) Recheck tire/fender clearances. This should be checked again after the load is in place. Repair if necessary.

10) Safety chain in place?

11) Each individual light working properly?

Refer to *TRAILERS—How to Tow and Maintain* for a more complete on-the-road checklist which includes the tow vehicle.

Building a trailer can be lots of fun but now that you're educated about it, you can see why we say a trailer is not just two wheels, an axle and a coupler to connect it to the tow vehicle.

APPENDIX

A. Suppliers & Manufacturers

B. References & Bibliography

C. Glossary of Trailer & Technical Terms

APPENDIX A
SUPPLIERS & MANUFACTURERS

Companies supplying catalogs for information and further study. Since many of these companies carry the same merchandise, finding and contacting the one closest to you is the easiest solution. Catalogs may require a small fee.

Suppliers/Distributors of Major Trailer Parts

Century Wheel & Rim . . . . **Catalog Price $3.75**
- 1550 Gage Road, Montebello, CA 90640 • (213) 728-3901 • Fresno, CA
- Hayward, CA • West Sacramento, CA • National City, CA • Phoenix, AZ

Northern Hydraulics . . . . **Catalog Price $FREE**
P. O. Box 1499   (_call for catalog or location of local store_)
Burnsville, Minnesota 55337-0499 • (800) 533-5545, in MN (612) 894-8310

Direct Line/Specialty Equipment . . . . **Catalog Price $FREE**
- 7721 Pillsbury Ave S, Richfield, Minnesota 55423 • (612) 452-9267

Quality Trailer Products . . . . **Catalog Price $5.00**
633 N.W. Parkway, Azle, Texas 76020 • (817) 444-1341, (817) 444-4518

Trailer Components of Florida . . . . **Catalog Price $5.00**
- 1020 S. 86th Street, Tampa, Florida • (813) 621-6968

Hayes Axle . . . . **Catalog Price $3.00**
- Little Rock, AK - (501) 568-5353 • McMinnville, OR - (503) 472-3196
- Seminole, OK - (405) 382-5150 • Ontario, CA - (909) 467-0113 • Elkhart, IN - (219) 294-6651

Redneck Trailer Supplies . . . . **Catalog Price $10.00**
- Springfield, MO • (417) 864-5210   (_request catalog or location of closest outlet_)

Portsmouth Trailer Supply . . . . **Catalog Price $FREE**
3227 South Military Highway, Chesapeake, Virginia 23323 • (804) 487-2934

Lucky Manufacturing . . . . **Catalog Price $8.00**
- P.O. Box 2278, Cookeville, TN • (615) 432-4034
- Boaz, AL - (205) 593-3984 • Fayetteville, PA - (717) 352-8544

Neiman's, Ltd . . . . **Catalog Price $10.00**
- RR1, P.O. Box 260, Industrial Park, Ventura, Iowa - (515) 829-3296
- 21840 Protecta Drive, Elkhart, Indiana - (219) 295-7743

Oakland Wheel & Rim . . . . **Catalog Price $3.00**
2442 Webster St, Oakland, California 94612 • (510) 452-6022

Jamestown Distributors/John Smith . . . . **Catalog Price $FREE**
Hwy 17 & 21, Gardens Corner, Rte 1, Box 375, SeaBrook, SC • (803) 846-9500

AgServ Western Sales . . . . **Catalog Price $CALL**
7279 N. Pacific Ave, P.O. Box 606, Livingston, CA 95334 • (510) 651-6660

Automatic Distributors . . . . **Catalog Price $FREE**
22 Target Circle, Bangor, ME 04401 • (207) 942-6769

Major Coupler/Jack/Accessory Manufacturers:

Dutton Lainson
    451 West Second Street, Hastings, Nebraska 68901 • (402) 462-4141

Atwood Mobile Products
    4750 Hiawatha Drive, Rockford, Illinois 61103 • (815) 877-7461

Hammerblow
    P.O. Box 419, Wausau, Wisconsin 54402-0419 • (715) 842-0561

Fulton Manufacturing
    P.O. Box 8, Mosinee, Wisconsin 54455-0008 • (715) 693-1700

Unique Functional Products
    135 Sunshine Lane, San Marcos, California 92069 • (619) 744-1610

Shelby Industries, Inc.
    175 McDaniel Road, P.O. Box 308, Shelbyville, KY 40066 • (502) 663-2040

Kodiak Trailer Components
    7600 Sand Drive, Fort Worth, Texas 76118 • (800) 756-3425

Torsion Suspension Manufacturers:

Al-Ko Kober Corp — 25784 Borg Road, Elkhart, Indiana 46514 • (219) 264-0631

Dexter Axle — 222 Collins Road, Elkhart, Indiana 46516 • (219) 295-1900

PDI -Torax — 7750 Hub Parkway, Cleveland, Ohio 44125

Henschen Industrial — 522 N Main St, Jackson Center, Ohio 45334 • (513) 596-6125

UCF Flexiride — 1025 Busch Hwy, Pennasauken, New Jersey 08110 • (609) 488-1800

Technical Book Suppliers:

Steve Smith Autosports — 239 S. Glassel, Orange, CA 92666 • (714) 639-7681

Motorbooks — 729 Prospect Ave, Osceola, Wisconsin 54020 • (715) 294-3345

Little Professor, Books-A-Million, Borders, Brodart, Barnes & Noble

Opamp Technical Books—1033 N. Sycamore, Los Angeles, Calif (213) 464-4322

Brown Books — 1517 San Jacinto, Houston, Texas 77002 • (713) 652-3937

Tattered Cover — 1628 - 16th Street, Denver, CO • (303) 322-1965

Breakthrough Publications — 310 N. Highland Ave, Ossining, NY 10562

Intertec Publications—PO Box 12901, Overland Park, KS 66282 •(800) 262-1954

J.F. Lincoln Arc Welding Foundation —
    22801 St. Claire Ave, Cleveland, OH 44117 • (216) 481-8100

American Welding Society—550 NW LeJeune, Miami, FL 33126 • (800) 443-9353

ASM Interlational — P.O. Box 473, Novelty, OH 44072 (800) 336-5152

ASME Publications — Box 2900, Fairfield, NJ 07007 • (800) 843-2763

Society of Automotive Engineers —
    400 Commonwealth, Warrendale, PA15096 • (412) 776-4970

Local College & University Bookstores — Check your *Yellow Pages*.

Wheel, Tire, Hub Manufacturers:

Greenball Corporation

2525 El Presidio Ave, Long Beach, California 90810 • (213) 636-2364

Trailer Mate Tires

3227 South Military Highway, Chesapeake, Virginia 23323 • (800) 854-4824

Kelsey-Hayes Wheel, Drum & Brake

5300T Livernois, Detroit, Michigan 48232 • (313) 895-5211

Armstrong Tires

P.O. Box 48, Armstrong, Iowa 50514 • (712) 864-3202

Wilton Corporation

Industrial Park, Winchester, Tennessee 37398 • (616) 967-1417

Steel Suppliers:

Steel Suppliers are divided into houses that handle specific kinds of steel:

1) Angle, bar, roll-formed shapes   2) Tubing houses
3) Sheet metal houses—shear and/or slit sheet, coil steel to size.
4) Sheet metal job shops—shear, bend and do other fabrication.

Large houses are nationwide and carry a wide variety of aluminum and steel. Offices for two of these companies are listed below:

Jorgensen Steel
- Los Angeles, CA
- Oakland, CA
- Phoenix, AZ
- Honolulu, HA
- Seattle, WA
- Denver, CO
- Houston, TX
- Dallas, TX
- Tulsa, OK
- Kansas City, MO
- St. Louis, MO
- Minneapolis, MN

Ryerson Steel
- Boston
- Buffalo
- Charlotte
- Chattanooga
- Chicago
- Cincinnati
- Cleveland
- Dallas
- Denver
- Detroit
- Houston
- Indianapolis
- Jersey City
- Kansas City
- Los Angeles
- Memphis
- Milwaukee
- Minneapolis
- Philadelphia
- Pittsburgh
- San Francisco
- Seattle
- Spokane
- St. Louis
- Tulsa
- Wallingford

Smaller local houses, such as listed below, can carry a wide variety of products, have equipment for fabrication and may be more helpful for smaller orders. Check *Yellow Pages* for local suppliers.

Island City Steel — 10213 N. McAllister, Island City, OR 97850 • (503) 963-5124

Any vendor wishing to be listed here should send a copy of your catalog to Techni-Visions for inclusion in future reprints. Please include a list of the products you manufacture, handle or distribute, along with current addresses and phone numbers of all branch offices. Thank you.

APPENDIX B

REFERENCES & BIBLIOGRAPHY

1. Blodgett, Omer W., *Design of Weldments*, Eighth Printing, 1976, James F. Lincoln Arc Welding Foundation, Cleveland, Ohio.

2. Jorgensen, Earle M., *Jorgensen Steel Stock List and Reference Book*, 1988, Los Angeles, California.

3. Richards, K.G., *Fatigue Strength of Welded Structures*, 1969, The Welding Institute, Abington Hall, Cambridge, England.

4. Finch, R. & Monroe, T., P.E., *Welder's Handbook*, 1985, HP books, Tucson, Arizona.

5. Souders, Mott, *The Engineer's Companion*, 1966, John Wiley & Sons, New York, N.Y.

6. Rossi, B. E., *Welding and Its Application*, 1941, McGraw-Hill Book Co., New York, New York.

7. Oberg, Erik & Jones, F.D., *Machinery's Handbook, 14th Edition*, 1949, The Industrial Press, New York, New York.

8. Alabama Metals Industries Corp., Brochure No. XM 2/89/3M, *Expanded Metal and Grating*, 1989, Birmingham, Alabama.

9. Superwinch Form No CG344, *Superwinch Catalog*, 1986, Putnam, Connecticut.

10. *McMaster Carr Supply Catalog, No. 94,* 1988, Santa Fe Springs, California.

11. Badland, B.J., M.I.Plant.E., *Building & Towing a Trailer*, 1980/81, Mechanical Services, Ltd, Bolton, England.

12. Timken Company, *Bearing Selection Handbook*, 1986, Timken Bearing Company, Canton, Ohio.

13. Department of the Navy, *Federal Specifications: Chains & Attachments, Welded & Weldless*, 1990, Number RR-C-271D.

14. British Broadcasting Company, Channel 2, *Top Gear*, March 7, 1991.

15. Dutton Lainson, *Wheel Bearing Protector Drawing*, Number LIT-52, 1975, Hastings, Nebraska.

16. Unique Functional Products, *Bearing Buddy Product Brochure*, 1990 apx, San Marcos, California.

17. Henschen Industrial, *Henschen Rubber Torsion Axles*, 1975 apx, Henschen Industrial, Jackson Center, Ohio.

18. Grogan, R.J., *An Investigator's Guide to Tire Failures*, 1986, Institute of Police Technology & Management, University of North Florida, Jacksonville, Florida.

19. Strasman, Peter G., et al, *Chevrolet & GMC Vans 1968 through 1987 Owners Workshop Manual*, 1987, Haynes Publications, Inc., Newberry Park, California.

20. Kushnerick, John P., et al, *Chilton Repair & Tune-Up Guide—Jeep Wagoneer/ Commando/Cherokee/Truck 1957-86,* 1986, Chilton Book Company, Radnor, Pennsylvania.

21. Lehigh/Rocappi, et al, *Toyota Tercel Service Manual—1980, 1981, 1982;* 1982, Robert Bentley, Inc., Cambridge, Massachusetts.

APPENDIX C

GLOSSARY OF TRAILER & TECHNICAL TERMS

ACCELERATION. A change in velocity (ft/sec) or speed, over a period of time. Carries the units of ft /sec/ sec or ft/sec^2.

AMPLITUDE. The maximum distance a pendulum, or any oscillating system, might swing.

ANGLE. A steel bar roll-formed while hot into a cross-sectional shape of a 90° angle.

ARTICULATED VEHICLE. A two-part vehicle that turns a corner by swivelling at a central point in its body.

AXLE. A steel bar or tube that extends the width of the trailer. It supports the entire framework and load. Also attaches to the springs and is fitted with hub, wheel and tire at its extremities.

BACKING PLATE. Carries the brake shoes and all the mechanism used to actuate the brakes. Bolts solidly onto a flange that is welded to the axle.

BEARINGS. Highly machined parts that fit between the hub and spindle. The bearings allow the hub and wheel to rotate accurately and securely about the spindle.

BED. A flat surface used to support the cargo placed on top of the trailer. CG or C.G. A commonly used abbreviation for *center of gravity*.

BUTT WELD. The weld connecting two pieces of steel (or other metal), placed end to end.

CG or C.G. A commonly used abbreviation for *center of gravity*.

CHANNEL. A steel bar having a cross-sectional shape of a "squared C" with 90° corners. The most common form is a shape roll-formed while hot. For thinner cross sections, it can be cold roll-formed or bent from a piece of sheet steel.

COGNIZANT. Aware, noticeable.

CONDUIT. A channel, tube or trough used to house or convey electrical wires or fluid.

CORNERING STIFFNESS. A ratio of lateral force to slip angle used in vehicle dynamics to more easily understand the forces associated with a tire during cornering.

COUPLER. The formed steel part that welds permanently to the trailer frame and fits over the trailer ball and clamps when the trailer is to be towed.

CRITICAL SPEED. The speed at which a tow-car and trailer become unstable. At all speeds above this point, the instability becomes worse.

DAMPING, NEGATIVE. An oscillating system whose oscillations increase in size is said to have *negative damping*.

DAMPING, POSITIVE. An oscillating system whose oscillations decrease in size is said to have *positive damping*. A shock absorber is an example of something designed to create *positive damping*.

DEGREE OF FREEDOM. A variable or quantity that changes with time. An automobile typically has four degrees of freedom.

DELINEATE. Emphasize and point out in unusually sharp and vivid terms.

DETRIMENTAL. Something that will cause damage or injury.

DISPROPORTIONATELY. The individual parts are out of proper relation to each other.

DOUBLER. A second thickness of steel used to reinforce an area such as a butt-welded connection.

EMPHASIZE. Stress.

EMPIRICAL. Relying on experience and observation alone often without regard for theory.

ERRONEOUS. In error; incorrect.

FENDER. A cover that fits over the top of the tires. It acts to catch mud, dirt and debris thrown up from the road. It may be made of rolled or flat formed metal, rubber, fiberglass or plastic.

FENDER SKIRT. The inside panel that attaches to the fender and the framework of the trailer. Prevents debris being thrown up from the road onto your cargo.

FILLET WELD. A weld used to join two pieces of metal placed at 90° to each other. Typically a weld found in a corner.

FOIST. To pass off as genuine something that is false.

GAIN. A ratio of input divided by output which is, roughly speaking, equal to the amplitude of an oscillation.

GUSSET. A triangular shaped piece of steel used to reinforce a connection that carries loads through a very sharp corner.

HEAT TREAT. A controlled process whereby a piece of steel is heated to certain high temperatures to change the properties of the piece. Cooling speed is also controlled.

HITCH. The steel framework that welds or bolts to the tow vehicle frame or bumper and carries the towing ball.

HITCH ANGLE. The angle of intersection between trailer center line and towcar center line.

HUB. A precision machined part that spins around the axle or spindle on bearings. The wheel and tire bolt to the hub.

HUB & DRUM. The drum is part of the brake system and contains the surface against which the brake shoes press for friction necessary to stop the trailer. The hub and drum are usually cast as one solid piece of steel.

HYPOTHESIS. A preliminary, tentative assumption which is then tested for its logic and empirical consequences.

ILK. Sort, kind.

INERTIA. A property of matter such that it remains at rest (or moving in a straight line) until acted upon by some external force. Mass times velocity.

INHERENT. An essential part of something without which the something would not be what it is.

IRREPUTABLE. Having a bad reputation.

KINETIC ENERGY. Energy associated with movement. One half mass times velocity.

LAG. A system's delay in responding to some input or disturbance.

LATERAL. Coming from or going to the side, sideways.

MAGNITUDE. A numerical quantitative measure expressed as a multiple of some standard unit.

MALADY. A disease or disorder.

MASS. A term commonly used in engineering and science. In simple terms, it is weight without the effect of gravity. The mass of an object will be the same on Pluto as it is on the Earth, while the weight will be different depending on the acceleration of gravity.

MOMENTUM. A number which gives a measure of the length of time to bring a moving body to a stop while it is under the action of a constant force.

MOMENT OF INERTIA. A number or property which gives a measure of the body's resistance to rotation.

NATURAL FREQUENCY. The frequency at which a system will continue to vibrate when it is disturbed, until it self-destructs.

OSCILLATION. The back and forth movement of something; such as a sine wave, a pendulum, even a trailer.

PARAMETER. A fixed quantity used in equations that does not vary with time, such as length, width, volume, etc. Whereas a *variable* does vary with time.

PERUSAL. To examine carefully with attention and in detail.

PHASE. If something moves *in phase* with system oscillation, it is moving back and forth at the same time. If it is *out of phase* it is moving opposite system oscillations.

PITCH. Rotation about a transverse axis. During braking, an automobile will pitch forward. In contrast, *yaw* is rotation about a vertical axis.

POTENTIAL ENERGY. The energy of a piece of matter due to its position.

PROPENSITY. An intense inclination.

PROSE. Ordinary spoken or written language in contrast to poetry.

PURPOSE-BUILT. Built for a specific reason and no other; i.e., a trailer built to haul a compressor is purpose-built for the compressor.

RECTIFY. To correct by removing errors.

RESTORING FORCE. A force which operates to restore oscillations to their zero point.

RIM. A term often used in place of the word wheel. Both refer to the steel part onto which the rubber tire is mounted.

ROLL. Rotation about a horizontal axis, as occurs to an automobile during cornering. (See YAW and PITCH).

RUNNER. A long steel part used on car carrying trailers to support the wheel of the vehicle riding on the trailer.

SHORE-UP. A slang term meaning to reinforce.

SHOT PEEN. A process whereby a weldment can be bombarded with tiny steel shot to reduce residual stresses and strengthen the part.

SLIP ANGLE. The angle between the direction of motion and the direction a tire is turned in a corner.

SPINDLE. A highly machined part that permanently attaches to or is part of the axle. The bearings that carry the hub are slid over this part.

SPRING. An elastic device that recovers its original shape after being depressed. On an auto or trailer frame, it is often a flat steel bar designed to cushion the frame and cargo from road bumps.

SPRING FITTINGS. The hardware used to attach the springs to the axle. The many parts are made of metal and formed or machined into U-bolts, nuts, washers, shackle bolts, links, hangers, eyes, rockers.

STEP NECK. A formed steel, patented part that positions the coupler above the plane of the trailer bed making it possible to construct the trailer with a very low bed and frame height and maintain the coupler at standard hitch ball heights.

SUBSEQUENT. Following after this.

SUBSTANTIATE. To establish with competent evidence.

SUCCINCTLY. Terse, brief and concise.

SWAY. That motion of a trailer and tow-car when it swings from side to side as it is being towed. This yaw involves both trailer and tow-car.

TANDEM. Refers to two. In the case of a trailer, this word means a two-axle trailer.

TIRE. The rubber part of the wheel/tire assembly that rolls on the ground, contains air and fits over the steel wheel or rim.

TONGUE LEG. The structural member that attaches the trailer bed or frame to the coupler.

TORSION SUSPENSION. A crank arm style suspension that contains the springing mechanism in the bar that crosses the trailer bed.

TUBING. A steel bar with a hole down its center. Can be round, square, rectangular and even some odd shapes.

VARIABLE. A quantity that may assume any one of a set of values and changes with time. Contrasts to *parameter* which does not change with time.

VECTOR. A quantity that has magnitude and direction. Often represented by an arrow oriented in the direction of the force its describing.

VELOCITY. Distance travelled per unit of time. Carries the units of ft/sec. or miles/hour.

WHEEL. The steel rim to which the rubber tire is mounted. The center part of the wheel bolts to the hub.

YAW. Rotation about a vertical axis. Also, to deviate from side to side. Sway is a specific form of *yaw* which also often includes roll. Conversely, *pitch* is rotation about a transverse axis and *roll* about a horizontal axis.

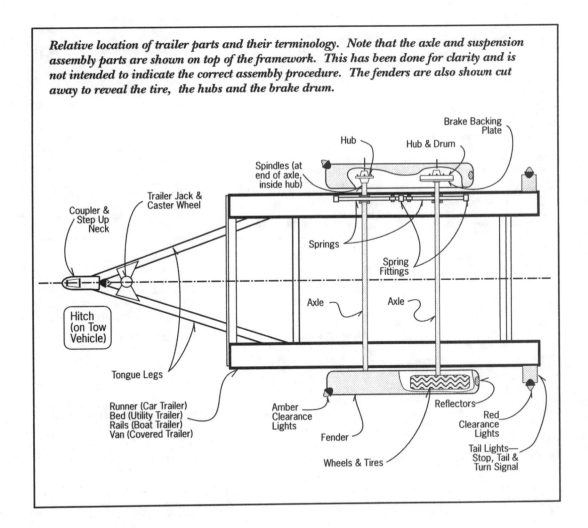

Relative location of trailer parts and their terminology. Note that the axle and suspension assembly parts are shown on top of the framework. This has been done for clarity and is not intended to indicate the correct assembly procedure. The fenders are also shown cut away to reveal the tire, the hubs and the brake drum.

INDEX

M

Magazines, 147
Magnesium, 17, 91, wheels, 91
Magnet, 92
Magnitude, 40
Main rails, 31, 39
Manufacture(d), 16, 48, 61, 69, 76, 97, 100, 113
Manufacturer(s), 31, 36, 47, 54, 59-61, 69, 73, 76, 79, 89-90, 97, 102, 110-111, 113, 115, 132, 141, 145, 147, 157, 160, 164
Manufacturing, 89, 150
Marker lights, 110
Mass, 14, 24, 45-46, 86, 142, 153
Massive, 15, 32, 34, 46-47, 151
Master cylinder, 94
Material(s), 1,3-4, 12-18, 24, 28, 30-32, 36, 38-40, 43-45, 60-61, 63, 65-66, 69, 75, 77-78, 97, 100, 104, 116-117, 123, 134, 137-139, 141, 143-144, 147-149, 151, 153, 155-158
Material size(s), 3, 17, 18, 65, 141,
Material stress, 17
McMaster Carr, 123, 134
Measure(d), 27, 37, 87-88, 138, 148,157
Measurements, 26, 36, 148
Measuring, 19, 36, 148
Mechanical, 57, 79, 91-92, 97-98, 122, 144, brakes, 91, 97-98, 122
Mechanically, 98
Mechanics, 97
Mechanism(s), 88, 94, 122, 128, 136
Melted, 42, 149-150, 153
Melting, 155
Melts, 155
Member(s), 18, 31, 38-39, 42, 61, 84, 94, 97, 119, 148, 157
Metal working, 125
Metals, 152, 160
Methods, 4, 14, 27, 40, 48, 68, 74, 89, 97, 104, 109, 113, 126, 135, 144, 150, 153, 157
MIG, 139, 153-156, welder, 154, welding, 139, 155
Mobile home, 38-39, 145, 147, 157
Model(s), 29, 38, 89
Modulus, section, 65
Molded rubber, 84, plugs, 116
Moment, 16-17, 61, 63-66, 71, 104, diagram(s), 61, 65, of inertia, 16-17, 63
Motor Vehicle Department, 2, 32
Motorhome, 92
Mounting(s), 30, 53, 61, 67, 73, 89, 96-97, 99, 101, 104-105, 109-112, 119, , 121, 127-129, 145, of lights, 110-112
Muriatic acid, 159

N

Neck(s), step, 16, 50, 52-53, 101
Negative camber, 85, 105-107
Net load, 38, 58-59
Nitrogen, 155
Non-locking nuts, 79
Non-rolling, 130

Nose, 47, 76, 92, 94, 97
Notched, 112
Notcher, 153
Numbering, 148
Numbers, 12, 26, 28, 40, 65, 73, 89, 148
Nut ringbolt, 133-134
Nylon closed end connectors, 118, 163

O

OD, 60
Offset(s), 61, 71, 89, 106, 127, 129
Offset: dimension, 106, loads, 127
Optimum strength, 17
Over-center, 132
Over-the-tongue, 138
Overall considerations, 23, 25, 27, 29, 31, 33, 35, 37, 39, 41, 43, 45, 47, 49, 51, 53, 55
Overhang, 5, 31, 44, 46, 60, 63, 65-66, 71, distance, 71
Overload(s), 27-28, 36, 38, 66, 76, 78, 88
Overloaded, 28, 36-37, 61, 76
Overloading, 38, 44, 61, 71
Overturn stability, 17
Oxidation, 155
Oxide, 160
Oxyacetylene, 149, 151, cutting torch, 151, torch, 149
Oxygen, 155, -acetylene, 151

P

P&O, 158-159
Padlock, 136
Paint(s), 45, 107, 157-161
Paint-Lok, 158
Painted, 90, 133, 160-161
Painting, 112, 143-144, 157-159, 161
Pallet, 131
Palletized, 132
Patented, 53, 86, 129, 133-134
Payload, 38
Pealing loads, 51, 97
Penetration, 69, 156-157
Perform(ance), 2, 5, 17, 24, 30, 48, 101
Performed, 61, 79, 145, 153
Performing, 32
Perpendicular, 44, 133, 148
Pickled and oiled, 158
Pigtail(s), 99, 107, 109, 116-117, 120, 161, 163, wires, 161
Pintle hook, 100-101
Placement, 2, 16, 22-24, 26, 31, 48, 53-54, 108, 111, 125, 133, 138, 148, 157-158
Plan(s), 2, 7, 20, 22, 61, 111, 141, 144, 152, 158
Planning, 3, 18, 31-32, 54, 144
Plasma cutter(s), 149, 151
Plastic, 109, 113, 116, 128, 159-160, bushing, 128, lights, 109
Plated, 79
Platform(s), 101, 137
Pliers, 118, 163
Plow steel, 63, 65-66

Plug(s), 107, 113, 116-117
Pockets, 140-141
Pony jack mount, 129
Positive camber, 105
Post(s), 128, 139-141
Power: hack saw, 149, hand shear, 152, shear(s), 149, 151-152
Precambered, 105
Predrilled, 60
Pressure relief valve, 74-75
Prices, 12, 109, 113, 115, 133
Primer(s), 159-160, coat, 160
Problem statement, 5-6
Proof test, 123
Properties, 13-14, 17, 39, 69, 78, 84
Proportions, 7, 46
Protect, 157-158, 160
Protected, 112, 159
Protecting, 74, 160
Protection, 42, 100, 111, 113, 116, 159
Protectors, bearing, 74-75
Psi, 63, 65-66
Purchasing, 69, 143-145, 147

R

Race(s), 25, 41, 71, 73, 131, 155-156
Rack jack, 126
Racks, 121-122, 125, 137, 140-142, 163-164
Radial tires (radials), 89
Radius, 87-88
Rails, 21, 31, 34, 39-40
Ramps, 32, 122
Ratchet, 132
Rating(s), 59, 61, 66, 73, 75-76, 78, 97, 100, 123, 127-128, 132, 145
Rating Life, 73
Ratio, 17, 46
Re-greasing, 74
Re-pack, 75
Re-packing, 74
Re-spray, 160
Re-tightened, 164
Re-weld, 75
Rear: lights, 111, overhang, 5, 31, 44, 46
Receptacle(s), 116-117, 128, 139-140
Rectangle, 22, 148
Rectangular, 21, 60, 139-140
Red oxide, 160
Reflectors, 111
Reinforce, 38, 79
Reinforcement(s), 32, 38
Reinforcing, 44
Rental, 92, 94, 101-102
Repair(s), 34, 43, 75, 79, 164
Repaired, 75
Research, 18, 110, 144
Resistor(s), selective, 93
Ribs, stiffener, 138
Rim(s), 60, 79,
Ring(s), 119-120, 134, 163
Ringbolt(s), nut, 133-134
Rivet(s), 40
Riveted, 128
Riveting, 139
Rocker(s), 79, 81, 88
Roll flexibility, 88
Roll-around dolly, 158

Roll-formed, 103
Roller, 73-74, 128
Rope(s), 130, 132, 136
Rotates, 84
Rotating, 150
Rotation, 74, 92, 97
Rough sketch, 7
Routing, 113, wires, 113
Rubber, 42, 84-88, 112, 116, 159-160
Rubber: grommet(s), 42, 112,
    suspension(s), 85
Rule(r), 7, 13, 54
Runner(s), 39
Runs, paint, 159-160
Rust inhibitive primer, 160
Rust(y), 71, 74, 94, 116, 119, 157-160

S

Saddle racks, 122, 137
Safety, 2, 16-17, 25-26, 112, 114, 121-
    125, 147, 150, 153, 158, 164,
    chain(s), 122-123, 124, 164,
    devices, 121-122, factor, 17
Sandblasting, 159
Sander, disc, 152
Sandpaper, 71
Saw blades, 149
Scale(s), 1, 4, 7-9, 18-21, 26, 148, 158-
    159
Scaling, 36
Scotch-lok(s), 163, 118
Screw(s), 111, 116, 118, 126
Section modulus, 65
Selecting, components, 1, 15, 57, 59,
    61, 63, 65, 67, 69, 71, 73, 75, 77,
    79, 81, 83, 85, 87, 89, 91, 93, 95,
    97, materials, 1, 13, scale, 1, 18
Selective resistor, 93
Semi-trailers, 117
Semi-trucks, 39
Serrated bolts, 79
Shackles, 106
Shape, 14, 16, 31, 39-40, 44, 46, 67, 79,
    103, 147, 149, 155, 158
Shear load(s), 16, 44
Shear(s), 16, 44, 61, 64, 133, 149, 151-
    153
Shearing, 145
Sheet, 3, 7, 17-18, 21, 138, 145, 147,
    149, 151-152, 158-159, metal, 145,
    147, 149, 151-152, steel, 138, 158
Short arc, 153,
Short: stiff springs, 29, tongue, 28, 43
Side loads, 127, 129
Side rack lift, 125
Side: rails, 67, truss, 32, view, 18, 21-
    22, 41-42, wind, 126-127
Sidewall(s), 89, 105-107, 125
Sideways force, 132
Six-volt battery, 93
Sizes, 1, 3, 15-16, 18, 31, 76-79, 81, 89,
    92, 101, 103, 122, 133, 139, 151-
    153
Sketch(es), 5, 7, 12, 18, 21
Sketching, 7
Slag, welding, 153
Sleeve, 159

Slip locks, 132
Slipper, 30, 77-82, spring(s), 77-78, 80,
    82, tube(s), 79, 81
Small load binders, 132
Solid bar axle, 60
Solvent(s), 71, 159
Spacers, wheel, 106-107
Spall, bearing, 73
Spindle(s), 16, 48, 57, 60, 61, 69-71, 73,
    75, 84-85, 89, 164
Spindle: nut, 68, strength, 71
Spindly, 28, 42, 45
Spoke wheels, 90, 136
Spot: welder, 156, welding, 138
Spray painting, 144, 158, 160
Spring(s), 7, 15, 26, 28-29, 30, 46, 57-
    61, 67, 69, 75-82, 84, 86-89, 106,
    116, 123, 126, 132, 145, 164
Spring: capacities, 78, centering holes,
    60, 68-69, centers, 60, hangers,
    145, hardware, 79-82, 145, pads,
    68-69, ratings, 78, scale, 26, sizes,
    77, U-bolts, 164, washers, 79
Spring eye(s), hardware, 79, 81
Springs, short stiff, 29
Spring-to-frame, 44
Square bend U-bolts, 133-134
Squareness, 148, 157
Stability, 16-17, 31, 48, 56, 89, 138
Stabilizer jacks, 125-127
Stake, 12, 139, 141
Stake-rack(s), 12, 139, 140-141
Stakeside(s), 121-122, 137, 139, 141
Standard, 30, 44, 48, 60, 66, 75, 77-78,
    80, 82, 88-90, 94, 100, 106, 120,
    140-141, 146
Standard: spring, 106, track, 60, two-eye
    spring(s), 77-78, 80, 82
State laws, 92, 123
State the problem, 1, 3, 5
Static, 67, 78, 88
Static: load, 67, 78, strength, 67
Station, 148
Steel, 3, 14-15, 17, 28, 32, 39, 45, 63,
    65-66, 78, 84-86, 90, 123, 128,
    132, 134, 138-140, 145, 147, 149-
    151, 153, 155, 158-160
Steel caster(s), 128, 158
Steel: eyebolts, 134, shapes, 14, 39,
    sheets, 139, slats, 139, torsion
    suspension(s), 85-86, wheels, 90
Step Neck™ (s), 16, 50, 52-53, 102
Steps to organization, 1-2, 18
Stick: welder, 154, welding, 153
Stiffener ribs, 138
Stiffeners, 16, 38, 139
Stiffness, 39, 86, 89-90
Straight, 4, 7, 17, 19, 42, 44, 46, 48, 60,
    62, 67, 100, 105, 122, 126, 145,
    148, 157, axle(s), 48, 62, 105, 145,
    tongues, 100
Stranded, 112, 163, wires, 163
Strap(s), 122, 132
Strength(s), 14, 16-17, 24, 30-32, 38-39,
    45-46, 61, 63, 67, 69, 71, 79, 123,
    125-126, 131, 133-134, 155, 157-
    158
Stress concentration(s), 40, 67, 69, 79
Stresses, 40, 63, 69
Stretch-out, 105
Stretched, 113

Stretches, 103
Stretching, 28, 88
Stripped, 163
Stripper(s), 161, 163
Stripping, 118, 161, 163, wires, 161
Structural, 24, 39, 42, 69, 84, 148
Structurally, 34-35, 52
Structure(s), 2, 23, 31, 34, 40, 45, 138,
    141, 155-157, 166
Superwinch, 130-131
Supplier, 15, 60, 79, 84, 89, 123, 145-
    146, 151, 160
Sure-Lube, 75
Surge, 92, 94-98, 122, actuator(s), 94-97,
    brakes, 122, hydraulic brakes, 92
Suspension(s), 12, 18, 22, 31-32, 34, 46,
    54, 57-60, 75-76, 78, 79, 80, 83-
    89, 91, 100, 106, 108, 120, 163
Suspension: style, 106, system(s), 57,
    76, 80, 91, 100, types, 57, 75
Suspension, conventional, 84, 88-89
Suspension, molded rubber, 84
Sway(ing), 13, 17, 24, 43, 47, 86, 92, 96
Swing-up, 126
Switch(es), 93, 107-108, 122, 130
Swivel, 125-129, jacks, 126-127, 129,
    mount(s), 126, 128
Synthetic reducer, 159

T

T-splicing, 163
T-square, 4
T-tongues, 28, 42-45, 47
Tack, 122, 141, 148, 157, 160, weld(s),
    148, 157, coat, 160
Tacked, 157
Tacking, 157
Tail, 28-29, 108-112, 114-115, 157,
    161, light(s), 108-111, 114, 115,
    157, 161
Tailgate(s), 21, 32, 122, 125, 137, 139
Tall hanger, 81
Tandem: axle, 78, 83, rocker, 81,
    suspension, 83, trailer(s), 54, 76,
    137
Tandem(s), 54-55, 76, 78, 80-81, 83,
    137, 160
Tank, 155
Tapered roller bearings, 73
Techni-Visions, 79, 129, 133, 158
Temperature(s), 74, 84, 149, 160
Tensile, 16-17, 63, strength, 16, stress,
    16-17, 63
Tension, 35, 60, 132, 134, springs, 132
Testing lab, 67, 86
Tests, 111
Thickness, 77-78, 113, 139, 153
Thinner, 159
Thread(ed), 106, 125, 133-134, 164
Threads, 69
Tie down(s), 121-122, 125, 131-133,
    135, hardware, 16, 21, 133, loops,
    132-134, straps, 122
Tire(s), 22, 28, 30-31, 34, 36, 38, 43,
    46-47, 57-61, 71, 79, 86, 89-91,
    101, 103, 105-107, 112, 133, 135-
    137, 141, 144, 158, 163-164
Tire: capacities, 90, capacity, 59,
    cornering stiffness, 86, racks, 137

TECHNI-VISIONS

publishes all these outstanding books about trailers:

TRAILERS—How to Tow & Maintain. Designed as an owner's manual, this book contains towing helps and cautions. Step by step procedures for thorough inspection and maintenance of a trailer are topped off with the most detailed Trouble Shooting guide for trailers yet published. ISBN 0-914483-15-3. . . . . $ 9.95

TRAILERS—How to Buy & Evaluate. Improve your chances of success in purchase of a trailer, selecting a hitch and setting up your tow vehicle and trailer. Real help in evaluating frameworks and understanding the causes of trailer sway—a full three chapters on each. Arranged and written in an easily readable manner, the subjects are basic for all designers, builders, buyers and users to understand. A simplified substitute for *Volumes 2* and *3* of *Design & Build*, described below. ISBN 0-914483-07-2 . . . . $12.95

TRAILERS—How to Design & Build. Building a trailer is a real challenge. This series of books reveals the tricks of the trade and considerations vital to success.

Volume 1. Basics. Planning a successful trailer requires more than just a fleeting thought. This book provides insight on all phases of construction. Basic components are discussed at length including suspension, axles, hubs, brakes, couplers, electrical and accessories. Factors important in helping you initiate a successful project are the core of this first in the series. ISBN 0-914483-31-5. . . . .$ 24.95

Volume 2. Structure. Designing a framework for adequate strength, without being overly heavy is an important step. This book discusses the various considerations and calculations necessary for selection of the appropriate materials. Welded and bolted joints are discussed along with a complete chapter on fatigue. ISBN 0-914483-32-3 . . . .$ 29.95

Volume 3. Performance. Towability is a fine art achieved by balancing a number of dimensions and factors. Calculations for center of gravity, moment of inertia, trailer sway and weight distribution are all discussed as part of understanding this complex dynamic requirement. *(available mid 2000).* ISBN 0-914483-33-1 . . . . $ 39.95

IRD Trailer Catalogs. Although IRD Trailers discontinued manufacturing trailers in 1986, the catalogs produced by *Techni-Visions* for IRD are still the most informative in the industry. The break-away drawings of *Utility Trailers* &/or *Car Trailers* alone are worth the price of the catalog to understand the parts required to build a trailer.

Utility Trailers Catalog . . . . $ 5.00

~~*Car Carrier~~ **SORRY, SOLD OUT** ~~. . $ 8.00~~

Check out availability at local book, trailer supply, hardware or automotive parts stores. Or order direct (with check or money order) from the address below. Be sure to include **Handling charges**—first book $ 3.00, additional books/catalogs, $2.00 each . Please add **8.25% tax** if you live in California.

TECHNI-VISIONS, 7621 E. Firestone Blvd, Suite E-11, Downey, CA, 90241 • (213) 460-2550

— 1998 —

TECHNI-VISIONS

7621 E. Firest[one] 90241 • (213) 460-2550

16100-A Garfield Ave
Paramount, CA 90723
(323) 460-2550

Buyer

Name _____

Address _____

City _____State____Zip_____

Phone _____

Ship to Address

Name _____

Address _____

City _____State____Zip_____

Phone _____

Qty	Item #	Title	Each	Total
	0-914483-15-3	*TRAILERS—How to Tow & Maintain*	$ 9.95	
	0-914483-07-2	*TRAILERS—How to Buy & Evaluate*	$12.95	
	0-914483-31-5	*TRAILERS—Design & Build. Vol 1. Basics*	$ 24.95	
	0-914483-32-3	*TRAILERS—Design & Build. Vol 2. Structure*	$ 29.95	
	0-914483-33-1	*TRAILERS—Design & Build. Vol 3. Performance**	$ 39.95	
	0-914483-08-0	*Car Carriers C* **SORRY SOLD OUT**	$ 8.00	
	0-914483-09-9	*Utility Trailers Catalog*	$ 5.00	

Merchandise Total =		
8.25% Tax (Calif residents only) on Subtotal above =		
Shipping & Handling, First Book =	$ 3.00	
S & H, each add'l book @ $2.00 each =		
Faster U.S. Delivery, add $4.00 =		
Canadian shipments, add $8.00 =		
Other =		
TOTAL =		

Vol 3. Performance. (avail mid 2000)

- Please allow 3 weeks for delivery in U.S.
- Prices and availability of books may change.
- Prices shown here are good through December 1998.

- Please send Cash or Money Order. Sorry, no COD's, no Bank Cards.
- Canada shipments, add $8.00. Other international orders, request quote.
- Libraries, schools, institutions, please send purchase order hard copy.